CONFIGURATIONS

TO MARIE-JOSÉ

UNESCO COLLECTION OF REPRESENTATIVE WORKS

This book
has been accepted
in the Latin American Series
of the Latin American Collection
of the United Nations
Educational, Scientific and Cultural Organization
(UNESCO)

The Collected Poems, 1957-1987
Configurations
A Draft of Shadows and Other Poems
Eagle or Sun?
Early Poems 1935-1955
Selected Poems
Sunstone
A Tree Within

Octavio Paz

CONFIGURATIONS

Translated from the Spanish by G. AROUL, PAUL BLACKBURN, LYSANDER KEMP, DENISE LEVERTOV, JOHN FREDERICK NIMS, MURIEL RUKEYSER, J. SWAMINATHAN, CHARLES TOMLINSON, MONIQUE FONG WUST and the author.

A New Directions Book

Library of Congress Catalog Card Number: 78-145932

ACKNOWLEDGEMENTS
Translation by Lysander Kemp from *Modern European Poetry,* copyright © 1966 by Bantam Books, Inc. Some of these poems and translations first appeared in *Artes Hispanicos, Delos, Hudson Review, Malahat Review, Mundus Artium,* and *Texas Quarterly.*

The translation of poetry for this volume was assisted by a grant from The Inter-American Foundation for the Arts and by the Center for Inter-American Relations, Inc.

Manufactured in the United States of America
New Directions books are printed on acid-free paper

First published clothbound (ISBN: 0-8112-0347-6) and as
New Directions Paperbook 303 (ISBN: 0-8112-0150-3) in 1971
Published simultaneously in Canada by Penguin Books Canada Limited.

New Directions Books are published for James Laughlin
by New Directions Publishing Corporation,
80 Eighth Avenue, New York 10011

TWELFTH PRINTING

INTRODUCTION

This book is by a world-poet who, in the decade into which we are invited, has reached the consciousness of readers at an extreme depth, stretched in suffering, power, phosphorescence, eroticism.

In a plunging, fiery gathering of the world under the Americas and Asia, under the cities of Europe, he holds the sea and the landscapes open: this woman, these streets, this night, the drums of sky and earth. He holds a recognizable world open to us, he offers it glittering; transparent; charred; and always made of flesh, even when it is made of myth.

His power has come through in this decade to readers of his poems and prose in English. You have here a next kind of man, long called-for, but never before existing. Octavio Paz is the poet who feeds deep under Indian and American life in all the Americas, and deep in the European tearing and fascination, making poems of this tradition; the man who knows Asia too, traveling within the Japan of Bashō and the Japan of this century, and within India, that world entire of teeming and of thirst, cities, caves, villages, all the postures of desire and rage, mountains to Ceylon.

In Spain during the Civil War, Octavio Paz returned to Mexico and from there went to California, where we first met in 1944 and where I began to translate his poems. He then went to New York (serving with the United Nations), to France, Japan, and back to Mexico. He stayed there for some years and left for the Mexican Embassy in Paris. Later he went as Ambassador to India. He married during his six years there, and wrote some of the latest poems in this book.

The long time in Europe and Asia, and always intent on Mexico—that is, his intentness went farther inward as he came to action in a life in which he could represent and express and make the gestures for what he believed, a life which he has only recently quit at a moment in which the depth of his poems and his action has been involved. I speak of his public life here, because Octavio Paz has lived in such a way that his life 'as poet' has been joined to his outward gestures, and, as I write this in Mexico City, it is felt at the depth by his readers in the United States and his readers in Mexico.

The writing of Octavio Paz has appeared here in several volumes: the poems in *Libertad bajo palabra* (1935–1957) and early translations of mine were gathered in *Selected Poems*, published by Indiana University Press; *The Labyrinth of Solitude* (1950), a book of essays which has been seminal in Mexico, was translated by Lysander Kemp and published here by Grove; a study of Claude Lévi-Strauss, translated by J. S. and Maxine Bernstein, has been published by Cornell University Press; *Eagle or Sun?*, prose poems translated by Eliot Weinberger and published by October House; *Sun Stone*, his cyclical poem, was published in my translation by New Directions and is included here with poems from *Salamandra* (1958–1961) and *Ladera este* (1962–1968), written in India. These recent poems mark the beginning of a new phase of Paz' work; other streams of his writing are in his prose works, essays, books of art criticism and literary criticism in *El arco y la lira* (1956), *Las peras del olmo* (1957), *Cuadrivio* (1965), *Puertas al campo* (1966), *Corriente alterna* (1967), *Marcel Duchamp* (1968), *Conjunciones y disyunciones* (1969) *and Posdata* (1970); works dealing with art, anthropology, philosophy, ethics; and his translations of Bashō, Nerval, Mallarmé, Pessoa, Apollinaire, Cummings, W. C. Williams. During 1968, he published two volumes of concrete poetry, *Topoemas* and *Discos visuales*.

Great incantations are here, like 'Salamander' and brilliant short lyrics from *Ladera este*, and poems that are letters to the composer John Cage and Leon Felipe: and the culminating poems, 'Wind from all Compass Points' and the new long poem, 'Blanco'. It opens with the epigraph, from a Tantra:

By passion the world is bound, by
passion too it is released.

The forces that unify this book are in the work itself, and in the driving forces behind the poems of Octavio Paz. I speak now of the other translators, and the qualities in their work. They are poets of the finest gifts, among them Denise Levertov, Lysander Kemp, Paul Blackburn, Charles Tomlinson. Often, editors avoid the inclusion of several hands in a work of translation; here, there is an additional interest, I think, because although the avenues of entrance are very different (and you will see how the sounds dance toward and away from the original webs of sound), there is a likeness of devotion and excitement that can be felt at once, and that makes its own kind of unity in this book.

'Sun Stone' opens this collection and is reprinted from the World Poets Series of a few years ago. This is a poem of opposites seen in a swift cycle: cypher of star, woman, season, the tree over water, graces and ferocities. All the shifts of experience, the acrobatics of inward turning, the bite and venom of the moment, are seen in a long period of 584 days —the 584 lines of the poem—as they are marked on the Aztec Calendar Stone.

The huge round wheel-stone can be seen in Mexico City, in what is certainly one of the most human beautiful places of the world. Here people go into a long, low building which suddenly appears as something quite else. You walk past this gate-building and see the second place ... like coming to the quiet sustained passage of a raga, to your second strength of listening, and through that entering the actual country of music ... or going into the contradictions of this poem, you may find (at whatever point this comes to you) the dance and point of breathing through which you move freely into the country of the opposites, where they merge and flow and sever again like daily life. Now, in the building in Mexico City, the Anthropological Museum, you see a lit country beyond the first low entrance. You see a tall pillar of carved stone, from whose widened top you realize there is water falling, freely, all around, onto an open space through which, without rims or walls, you walk. Behind this mushroom, this fountain of experience, are many houses of the building, houses of the gifts of all people to each other, and of the wars between the gifts. On the walls of one such is the Stone for which Octavio Paz' poem is named.

In the city beyond all of this, the awareness of Paz is now like the aware-ness of Lorca; or of Darío and Amado Nervo. With this difference: people here can say poems of Lorca's, the son of the house, the candy-woman at the corner of the plaza. Paz' poems are loved and used also, by the people in Mexico City, the students of the university, saying and using his famous lines from *The Broken Jar*:

> we have to dream further, all the way to the
>   fountain, we have to row centuries upstream,
> further than infancy, further than the beginning,
>   further than the baptizing waters,
> to throw down walls between person and person, to
>   join anew that which is separated,
> life and death are not worlds opposite, they are
>   one single stalk with two twin flowers
> we have to dig up the lost word ...
> to decipher the tattooing on night and look
>   face to face at noon and tear its mask away

These lines are now printed again, in the students' journal, with the open, loving faces of a young man and a young woman. And people at a hotel say: Is Paz coming back to Mexico?

This is the event which has joined his life and his poems in a new way to us and to the Mexicans: in the autumn of 1968, when a demonstration of students was attacked by force, from helicopters, with guns, with tanks, many students were imprisoned, many wounded, and an un-counted number killed. The story in Mexico says that their bodies were incinerated, and no report was made to their families or in the press.

At this moment, Octavio Paz was asked, as many poets were, to send a poem to the cultural committee of the Olympic Games, which were just about to be held in Mexico City, and which the commercial and political groups felt were being threatened by the reality of the students' struggle.

Paz renounced his embassy and sent this poem, of clarity, cleanness, clearness, and everything limpid in itself or washed by everything hired to make it clean. The Spanish word 'limpidez' has all of these meanings in it, it goes from the abstract purity to the washerwoman's purity. Paz dedicates the poem to Dore and Adja Yunkers, and asks that it be given to the poets who were to be present at the Olympiad meeting, telling them that the recent turn of events had made him change his mind and to send a poem, after his earlier decision not to participate.

'La limpidez' the poem begins in clarity and cleanness,

> (Maybe it's worth it
> To write this on the cleanness
> Of this sheet)
> > It is not clean:
> It is a rage
> > (Yellow and black
> Accretion of bile in Spanish)
> Reaching across the page.
> Why?
> > *Shame is anger*
> *Turned against oneself*:
> > > *If*
> *A whole nation come to shame*
> *It is a lion crouching*
> *For the leap.*
> > (The municipal
> Employees are washing the blood
> Away in the Plaza de los Sacrificios.)
> Look at it,
> > Stained
> Before saying anything
> Worth it,
>
> > La limpidez.
>
> > Delhi, October 3 1968

One more word: the erotic strength of Paz is never separated from the rest, as it has been in the writing of many contemporaries who tear all things from all things. Paz is one of the great erotic writers, yes; it hardly needs to be said. He has written, in front of his book *Homages and Profanations*: 'If eroticism belongs to all ages and all civilizations, love itself is a western passion. Like everything we have invented ... ' and then he speaks of contradiction that cannot be resolved without destroying or transfiguring, image-making. 'Images of love, transfigurations of passion: poems. ... Profanations and homage.'

MURIEL RUKEYSER

Mexico City—New York, January 1969

Contents

Piedra de Sol/Sun Stone
(1957)

Piedra de Sol

un sauce de cristal, un chopo de agua,
un alto surtidor que el viento arquea,
un árbol bien plantado mas danzante,
un caminar de río que se curva,
avanza, retrocede, da un rodeo
y llega siempre:
                        un caminar tranquilo
de estrella o primavera sin premura,
agua que con los párpados cerrados
mana toda la noche profecías,
unánime presencia en oleaje,
ola tras ola hasta cubrirlo todo,
verde soberanía sin ocaso
como el deslumbramiento de las alas
cuando se abren en mitad del cielo,

un caminar entre las espesuras
de los días futuros y el aciago
fulgor de la desdicha como un ave
petrificando el bosque con su canto
y las felicidades inminentes
entre las ramas que se desvanecen,
horas de luz que pican ya los pájaros,
presagios que se escapan de la mano,

una presencia como un canto súbito,
como el viento cantando en el incendio,
una mirada que sostiene en vilo
al mundo con sus mares y sus montes,
cuerpo de luz filtrada por un ágata,
piernas de luz, vientre de luz, bahías,
roca solar, cuerpo color de nube,

Sun Stone

willow of crystal, a poplar of water,
a pillar of fountain by the wind drawn over,
tree that is firmly rooted and that dances,
turning course of a river that goes curving,
advances and retreats, goes roundabout,
arriving for ever:
                the calm course of a star
or the spring, appearing without urgency,
water behind a stillness of closed eyelids
flowing all night and pouring out prophecies,
a single presence in the procession of waves,
wave over wave until all is overlapped,
in a green sovereignty without decline
a bright hallucination of many wings
when they all open at the height of the sky,

course of a journey among the densities
of the days of the future and the fateful
brilliance of misery shining like a bird
that petrifies the forest with its singing
and the annunciations of happiness
among the branches which go disappearing,
hours of light even now pecked away by the birds,
omens which even now fly out of my hand,

an actual presence like a burst of singing,
like the song of the wind in a burning building,
a long look holding the whole world suspended,
the world with all its seas and all its mountains,
body of light as it is filtered through agate,
the thighs of light, the belly of light, the bays,
the solar rock and the cloud-coloured body,

3

color de día rápido que salta,
la hora centellea y tiene cuerpo,
el mundo ya es visible por tu cuerpo,
es transparente por tu transparencia,

voy entre galerías de sonidos,
fluyo entre las presencias resonantes,
voy por las transparencias como un ciego,
un reflejo me borra, nazco en otro,
oh bosque de pilares encantados,
bajo los arcos de la luz penetro
los corredores de un otoño diáfano,

voy por tu cuerpo como por el mundo,
tu vientre es una plaza soleada,
tus pechos dos iglesias donde oficia
la sangre sus misterios paralelos,
mis miradas te cubren como yedra,
eres una ciudad que el mar asedia,
una muralla que la luz divide
en dos mitades de color durazno,
un paraje de sal, rocas y pájaros
bajo la ley del mediodía absorto,

vestida del color de mis deseos
como mi pensamiento vas desnuda,
voy por tus ojos como por el agua,
los tigres beben sueño en esos ojos,
el colibrí se quema en esas llamas,
voy por tu frente como por la luna,
como la nube por tu pensamiento,
voy por tu vientre como por tus sueños,

tu falda de maíz ondula y canta,
tu falda de cristal, tu falda de agua,
tus labios, tus cabellos, tus miradas,
toda la noche llueves, todo el día
abres mi pecho con tus dedos de agua,
cierras mis ojos con tu boca de agua,

4

colour of day that goes racing and leaping,
the hour glitters and assumes its body,
now the world stands, visible through your body,
and is transparent through your transparency,

I go a journey in galleries of sound,
I flow among the resonant presences
going, a blind man passing transparencies,
one mirror cancels me, I rise from another,
forest whose trees are the pillars of magic,
under the arches of light I go among
the corridors of a dissolving autumn,

I go among your body as among the world,
your belly the sunlit centre of the city,
your breasts two churches where are celebrated
the great parallel mysteries of the blood,
the looks of my eyes cover you like ivy,
you are a city by the sea assaulted,
you are a rampart by the light divided
into two halves, distinct, colour of peaches,
and you are saltiness, you are rocks and birds
beneath the edict of concentrated noon,

and dressed in the colouring of my desires
you go as naked as my thoughts go naked,
I go among your eyes as I swim water,
the tigers come to these eyes to drink their dreams,
the humming-bird is burning among these flames,
I go upon your forehead as on the moon,
like cloud I go among your imagining
journey your belly as I journey your dream,

your loins are harvest, a field of waves and singing,
your loins are crystal and your loins are water,
your lips, your hair, the looks you give me, they
all night shower down like rain, and all day long
you open up my breast with your fingers of water,
you close my eyelids with your mouth of water,

sobre mis huesos llueves, en mi pecho
hunde raíces de agua un árbol líquido,

voy por tu talle como por un río,
voy por tu cuerpo como por un bosque,
como por un sendero en la montaña
que en un abismo brusco se termina
voy por tus pensamientos afilados
y a la salida de tu blanca frente
mi sombra despeñada se destroza,
recojo mis fragmentos uno a uno
y prosigo sin cuerpo, busco a tientas,

corredores sin fin de la memoria,
puertas abiertas a un salón vacío
donde se pudren todos los veranos,
las joyas de la sed arden al fondo,
rostro desvanecido al recordarlo,
mano que se deshace si la toco,
cabelleras de arañas en tumulto
sobre sonrisas de hace muchos años,

a la salida de mi frente busco,
busco sin encontrar, busco un instante,
un rostro de relámpago y tormenta
corriendo entre los árboles nocturnos,
rostro de lluvia en un jardín a oscuras,
agua tenaz que fluye a mi costado,

busco sin encontrar, escribo a solas,
no hay nadie, cae el día, cae el año,
caigo con el instante, caigo a fondo,
invisible camino sobre espejos
que repiten mi imagen destrozada,
piso días, instantes caminados,
piso los pensamientos de mi sombra,
piso mi sombra en busca de un instante,

busco una fecha viva como un pájaro,
busco el sol de las cinco de la tarde

6

raining upon my bones, and in my breast
the roots of water drive deep a liquid tree,

I travel through your waist as through a river,
I voyage your body as through a grove going,
as by a footpath going up a mountain
and suddenly coming upon a steep ravine
I go the straitened way of your keen thoughts
break through to daylight upon your white forehead
and there my spirit flings itself down, is shattered
now I collect my fragments one by one
and go on, bodiless, searching, in the dark,

the limitless corridors of memory
the doors that open on empty living-rooms
where every springtime withers and rots away
the jewels of thirst are burning at the base,
the face obliterated at memory,
the hand which will dissolve if I even touch it,
threads of those spider-webs in chaos over
the smiling of a past that falls away,

I search where I come face to face with daylight,
search without finding, I search for a moment,
for a face of lightning-flash and thunderstorm
running among the enormous trees of night,
face of all rain in a garden of shadows,
insistent water that flows along my side,

I search without finding, and I write alone,
no one is here, and the day ends, the year ends,
I have gone down with the moment, all the way down,
the road is invisible over all these mirrors,
they repeat and reflect for ever my broken image,
I pace the days, the moments pave this roadway,
I step upon the thinking of my shadow,
I pace my shadow in search of my one moment,

I seek the day live as a live bird,
I seek the five o'clock sun of afternoon

templado por los muros de tezontle:
la hora maduraba sus racimos
y al abrirse salían las muchachas
de su entraña rosada y se esparcían
por los patios de piedra del colegio,
alta como el otoño caminaba
envuelta por la luz bajo la arcada
y el espacio al ceñirla la vestía
de una piel más dorada y transparente,

tigre color de luz, pardo venado
por los alrededores de la noche,
entrevista muchacha reclinada
en los balcones verdes de la lluvia,
adolescente rostro innumerable,
he olvidado tu nombre, Melusina,
Laura, Isabel, Perséfona, María,
tienes todos los rostros y ninguno,
eres todas las horas y ninguna,
te pareces al árbol y a la nube,
eres todos los pájaros y un astro,
te pareces al filo de la espada
y a la copa de sangre del verdugo,
yedra que avanza, envuelve y desarraiga
al alma y la divide de sí misma,

escritura de fuego sobre el jade,
grieta en la roca, reina de serpientes,
columna de vapor, fuente en la peña,
circo lunar, peñasco de las águilas,
grano de anís, espina diminuta
y mortal que da penas inmortales,
pastora de los valles submarinos
y guardiana del valle de los muertos,
liana que cuelga del cantil del vértigo,
enredadera, planta venenosa,
flor de resurrección, uva de vida,
señora de la flauta y del relámpago,
terraza del jazmín, sal en la herida,
ramo de rosas para el fusilado,

8

tempered red by the red walls of *tezontle*:
an afternoon hour, ripening its clusters,
and as it bursts the girls emerge in light
from that rose-coloured centre and they scatter
out from the terrace of the college building,
tall as the autumn one girl walking onward
involved in light among the far arcades
and space girdles her round in a bright garment
of a new body more golden and transparent,

a tiger the colour of light, a dark-brown deer
loping along the outskirts of the night,
a girl glimpsed once as she that once reclined
along the greenest balconies of the rain,
the endless unnumbered adolescent face,
I have forgotten your name, was it Melusine,
Laura, Isabel, Mary, Persephone,
your face is all their faces and none of them,
you are all the times and never any of them,
you take on the likeness of a tree, a cloud,
you are all birds and now you are a star,
now you resemble the sharp edge of a sword
and now the executioner's bowl of blood,
the encroaching ivy that overgrows and then
roots out the soul and divides it from itself,

writing of fire on the slab of jade,
the cleft in the rock, serpent-goddess and queen,
pillar of cloud, and fountain struck from the stone,
the nest of eagles, the circle on the moon,
the seed of anise, mortal and smallest thorn
that has the power to give immortal pain,
shepherd of valleys underneath the sea
and guardian of the valley of the dead,
liana that hangs at the pitch of vertigo,
climber and bindweed and the venomous plant,
flower of resurrection and grape of life,
lady of the flute and of the lightning-flash,
terrace of jasmine, and salt rubbed in the wound,
a branch of roses for the man shot down,

nieve en agosto, luna del patíbulo,
escritura del mar sobre el basalto,
escritura del viento en el desierto,
testamento del sol, granada, espiga,

rostro de llamas, rostro devorado,
adolescente rostro perseguido
años fantasmas, días circulares
que dan al mismo patio, al mismo muro,
arde el instante y son un solo rostro
los sucesivos rostros de la llama,
todos los nombres son un solo nombre,
todos los rostros son un solo rostro,
todos los siglos son un solo instante
y por todos los siglos de los siglos
cierra el paso al futuro un par de ojos,

no hay nada frente a mí, sólo un instante
rescatado esta noche, contra un sueño
de ayuntadas imágenes soñado,
duramente esculpido contra el sueño,
arrancado a la nada de esta noche,
a pulso levantado letra a letra,
mientras afuera el tiempo se desboca
y golpea las puertas de mi alma
el mundo con su horario carnicero,

sólo un instante mientras las ciudades,
los nombres, los sabores, lo vivido,
se desmoronan en mi frente ciega,
mientras la pesadumbre de la noche
mi pensamiento humilla y mi esqueleto,
y mi sangre camina más despacio
y mis dientes se aflojan y mis ojos
se nublan y los días y los años
sus horrores vacíos acumulan,

mientras el tiempo cierra su abanico
y no hay nada detrás de sus imágenes
el instante se abisma y sobrenada

snowstorm in August, moon of the harrowing,
the writing of the sea cut in basalt,
the writing of the wind upon the desert,
testament of the sun, pomegranate, wheat-ear,

a face of flames, face that is eaten away,
the adolescent and persecuted face
the years of fantasy and circular days
that open upon the same street, the same wall,
the moment flares up and they are all one face,
the procession of faces of this calling,
all of these names are unified in one name,
all of these faces are now a single face,
all centuries are now a single instant
and throughout the centuries of centuries
the path to the future shut by these two eyes,

there is nothing before me, but a moment
recovered tonight, standing against a dream
that is dreamed of images all intertwined,
sculptured in permanence against the dream:
a moment torn from the zero of this night,
lifted up forcibly, feature by feature,
meanwhile, beyond it, time, spilling its guts,
and hammering, banging on the doors of my soul,
the world, with its blood-spattered calendar,

only a moment while the capitals,
the names, strong flavours, the brightness of all things
crumble away within my sightless forehead,
while the mute heavy grieving of the night
beats down my thinking and my skeleton
and my blood courses more deliberately
and now my teeth begin to relent, my eyes
begin to cloud over; and the days and years
go heaping up their high and empty horrors,

time in an ancient gesture folds its fan
and there is nothing behind its images
the moment plunges into itself and floats

rodeado de muerte, amenazado
por la noche y su lúgubre bostezo,
amenazado por la algarabía
de la muerte vivaz y enmascarada
el instante se abisma y se penetra,
como un puño se cierra, como un fruto
que madura hacia dentro de sí mismo
y a sí mismo se bebe y se derrama
el instante translúcido se cierra
y madura hacia dentro, echa raíces,
crece dentro de mí, me ocupa todo,
me expulsa su follaje delirante,
mis pensamientos sólo son sus pájaros,
su mercurio circula por mis venas,
árbol mental, frutos sabor de tiempo,

oh vida por vivir y ya vivida,
tiempo que vuelve en una marejada
y se retira sin volver el rostro,
lo que pasó no fue pero está siendo
y silenciosamente desemboca
en otro instante que se desvanece:

frente a la tarde de salitre y piedra
armada de navajas invisibles
una roja escritura indescifrable
escribes en mi piel y esas heridas
como un traje de llamas me recubren,
ardo sin consumirme, busco el agua,
y en tus ojos no hay agua, son de piedra,
y tus pechos, tu vientre, tus caderas
son de piedra, tu boca sabe a polvo,
tu boca sabe a tiempo emponzoñado,
tu cuerpo sabe a pozo sin salida,
pasadizo de espejos que repiten
los ojos del sediento, pasadizo
que vuelve siempre al punto de partida,
y tú me llevas ciego de la mano
por esas galerías obstinadas
hacia el centro del círculo y te yergues

encircled by death among the threatenings
of the enormous mournful yawn of midnight,
and wholly threatened by the hullabaloo
of death enlivened by energy and masked,
the moment plunges and it pierces itself,
closes as a fist closes, like a perfect
fruit that ripens inwards in its own good time
spontaneously, drinks itself, and scatters,
the numinous moment shines, pierces itself,
and ripens inward, ripens and puts forth roots,
it grows within me, it completely fills me,
lavishes out on me delirious branches,
the thoughts flying within me are its birds,
and in my veins its mercury circulates,
the tree of the mind, its fruit tasting of time,

and life! to be lived, vivid nevertheless,
time that turns into a great surf approaching,
withdrawing without ever turning back,
the past is not the past, but it is here, now,
and in the silence of the present, it fills
into another moment which vanishes:

facing an afternoon, stone and saltpetre,
an enormous fleet of invisible razors,
you write a red and indecipherable
writing upon my skin and these open wounds
cover my body, a burning suit of flame,
I burn and am not consumed, I long for water,
and in your eyes there is no water, but stone,
your breasts are stone, your belly is stone, your loins
are made of stone, your mouth has the taste of dust,
your mouth tastes to me of an envenomed time,
your body has the taste of a pit without
any exit, a hall of mirrors reflecting
the eyes of one thirsty man, a corridor
returning for ever to its starting point,
and I in blindness, you take me by the hand
along these endless obstinate galleries
into the centre of this circle; erect,

como un fulgor que se congela en hacha,
como luz que desuella, fascinante
como el cadalso para el condenado,
flexible como el látigo y esbelta
como un arma gemela de la luna,
y tus palabras afiladas cavan
mi pecho y me despueblan y vacían,
uno a uno me arrancas los recuerdos,
he olvidado mi nombre, mis amigos
gruñen entre los cerdos o se pudren
comidos por el sol en un barranco,

no hay nada en mí sino una larga herida,
una oquedad que ya nadie recorre,
presente sin ventanas, pensamiento
que vuelve, se repite, se refleja
y se pierde en su misma transparencia,
conciencia traspasada por un ojo
que se mira mirarse hasta anegarse
de claridad:
                    yo vi tu atroz escama,
Melusina, brillar verdosa al alba,
dormías enroscada entre las sábanas
y al despertar gritaste como un pájaro
y caíste sin fin, quebrada y blanca,
nada quedó de ti sino tu grito,
y al cabo de los siglos me descubro
con tos y mala vista, barajando
viejas fotos:
                    no hay nadie, no eres nadie,
un montón de ceniza y una escoba,
un cuchillo mellado y un plumero,
un pellejo colgado de unos huesos,
un racimo ya seco, un hoyo negro
y en el fondo del hoyo los dos ojos
de una niña ahogada hace mil años,

miradas enterradas en un pozo,
miradas que nos ven desde el principio,
mirada niña de la madre vieja

you stand like lightning frozen into an axe,
the flaying light drawing and fascinating
as the built scaffold of death to the condemned,
flexible as a braided whip and slender
a twin weapon, a weapon like the moon,
and keenness of your speaking penetrates
my breast, leaving me empty and desolate,
you rip up all my memories by the roots,
I have forgotten my name, and now my friends
go grunting among the hogs, or lie and rot
eaten by the sun, beneath the precipice,

now there is nothing in me but one vast wound,
a gap with no possible way of healing,
a now without windows, a turn of intellect
moving on itself, repeating and reflecting,
it loses itself in its own transparency,
self-knowledge that is shot through by the eye
that watches itself watching, drowning itself
in clarity:
              I saw your frightful armour,
Melusine, at dawn, in your green scales burning,
you slept, in coils and entangled with the sheets,
and like a bird you shrieked on awakening
whitened and dwindled away, endlessly, broken,
nothing remained of you except that shrieking,
and at the end of the years, I find myself
with a cough and poor eyesight, turning over
old photographs:
                  nobody, you were no one,
nobody, a heap of ashes and a broom,
a knife with a notched edge, a feather duster,
a few feet of skin suspended on some bones,
a dried-out bunch of something, a black hole
and there at the bottom of the hole two eyes
eyes of a girl drowned a thousand years ago,

those looks buried at the bottom of the pit,
looking at us from the beginning of time,
the young girl in her seeing an old mother

que ve en el hijo grande un padre joven,
mirada madre de la niña sola
que ve en el padre grande un hijo niño,
miradas que nos miran desde el fondo
de la vida y son trampas de la muerte
—o es al revés: caer en esos ojos
es volver a la vida verdadera?,

—caer, volver, soñarme y que me sueñen
otros ojos futuros, otra vida,
otras nubes, morirme de otra muerte!
—esta noche me basta, y este instante
que no acaba de abrirse y revelarme
dónde estuve, quién fui, cómo te llamas,
cómo me llamo yo:
                              —hacía planes
para el verano —y todos los veranos—
en Christopher Street, hace diez años,
con Filis que tenía dos hoyuelos
donde bebían luz los gorriones?,
—por la Reforma Carmen me decía
'no pesa el aire, aquí siempre es octubre',
o se lo dijo a otro que he perdido
o yo lo invento y nadie me lo ha dicho?,
—caminé por la noche de Oaxaca,
inmensa y verdinegra como un árbol,
hablando solo como el viento loco
y al llegar a mi cuarto —siempre un cuarto—
no me reconocieron los espejos?,
—desde el hotel Vernet vimos al alba
bailar con los castaños —'ya es muy tarde'
decías al peinarte y yo veía
manchas en la pared, sin decir nada?,
—subimos juntos a la torre, vimos
caer la tarde desde el arrecife?,
—comimos uvas en Bidart?, —compramos
gardenias en Perote?,
                              nombres, sitios,
calles y calles, rostros, plazas, calles,
estaciones, un parque, cuartos solos,

who sees within her grown son a young father,
the mother's seeing of a lonely daughter
who sees in the kingly father a young son,
looks that look into us to the furthest depth
of life, that are the traps and snares of death
—is it the opposite? is falling in those eyes
the way back to the true and central life?

to fall, to return, to dream, and let me be
the dream of the eyes of the future, another life,
other clouds, and die at last another death!
—tonight is my life, and this single moment
which never stops opening, never stops revealing
where my life lay, who I was, what your name is
and what my own name is:
                                    was it I planning
for summer coming—and all coming summers—
in Christopher Street—this was ten years ago—
with Phyllis in the bright hollows of whose throat
the sparrows could come to drink, drinking the light?
on the Reforma did Carmen say to me
'this air is dry, it's always October here',
or did the other one say that, the one I lost,
or did I invent it, did nobody say it to me?
Was it I riding through a Oaxaca night
that was black-green and enormous, like a tree,
soliloquizing like the fantastic wind;
coming back to my room—always a room somewhere—
could the mirrors really not recognize me?
at the Hotel Vernet did we see dawn
dance with the chestnut trees—'it's late already'—
and did you do your hair and did I watch
the stains on the wall without saying a word?
did we go up the tower together, and see
the day descending on the outer reef?
did we eat grapes at Bidart? was it we
buying gardenias at Perote?
                                    names, places,
streets and streets, faces, streets, circles,
railway stations, a park, the single rooms,

manchas en la pared, alguien se peina,
alguien canta a mi lado, alguien se viste,
cuartos, lugares, calles, nombres, cuartos,

Madrid, 1937,
en la Plaza del Angel las mujeres
cosían y cantaban con sus hijos,
después sonó la alarma y hubo gritos,
casas arrodilladas en el polvo,
torres hendidas, frentes escupidas
y el huracán de los motores, fijo:
los dos se desnudaron y se amaron
por defender nuestra porción eterna,
nuestra ración de tiempo y paraíso,
tocar nuestra raíz y recobrarnos,
recobrar nuestra herencia arrebatada
por ladrones de vida hace mil siglos,
los dos se desnudaron y besaron
porque las desnudeces enlazadas
saltan el tiempo y son invulnerables,
nada las toca, vuelven al principio,
no hay tú ni yo, mañana, ayer ni nombres,
verdad de dos en sólo un cuerpo y alma,
oh ser total ...
           cuartos a la deriva
entre ciudades que se van a pique,
cuartos y calles, nombres como heridas,
el cuarto con ventanas a otros cuartos
con el mismo papel descolorido
donde un hombre en camisa lee el periódico
o plancha una mujer; el cuarto claro
que visitan las ramas del durazno;
el otro cuarto: afuera siempre llueve
y hay un patio y tres niños oxidados;
cuartos que son navíos que se mecen
en un golfo de luz; o submarinos:
el silencio se esparce en olas verdes,
todo lo que tocamos fosforece;
mausoleos del lujo, ya roídos
los retratos, raídos los tapetes;

stains on the wall, somebody combing her hair,
somebody singing beside me, somebody dressing,
rooms, places, streets, names, rooms,

Madrid, nineteen hundred and thirty-seven,
on the Plaza del Angel seeing the women
doing their sewing and singing with their sons,
and then the shriek of the siren and their shriek,
houses brought down and crawling in the dust,
the towers cloven, the faces running spittle
and the hurricane of engines, I hold static:
two naked people loving one another
for the sake of defending our eternal portion,
our rationing of time and of paradise,
to touch our root, to reach ourselves in touching,
to recover our inheritance pirated
by robbers of life in a thousand centuries,
these two took their clothes off and they kissed
because these nakednesses, woven together,
can overleap time and are invulnerable,
nothing can touch them, they go to the origins,
there is no You nor I, tomorrow, yesterday, names,
there truly two become only one body and soul,
O total being ...
                    there are rooms that are adrift
among the great cities that go foundering,
furnished rooms, city streets, names striking like wounds,
the room whose windows look out on other rooms
all papered in the same discoloured paper
where a man in shirt-sleeves reads his newspaper
or a woman irons; the room lit bright in spring
and, entering, the branches of the peach tree;
the other room: outside it is always raining,
there is a courtyard with three rusted children,
rooms that are ships, and that are rocking and singing
in a gulf of brilliance; or the submarines:
silence dispersed upon the greenness of waves
and everything that we touch phosphoresces;
memorials to a luxury whose pictures
are eaten away over the threadbare carpets;

trampas, celdas, cavernas encantadas,
pajareras y cuartos numerados,
todos se transfiguran, todos vuelan,
cada moldura es nube, cada puerta
da al mar, al campo, al aire, cada mesa
es un festín; cerrados como conchas
el tiempo inútilmente los asedia,
no hay tiempo ya, ni muro: —espacio, espacio,
abre la mano, coge esta riqueza,
corta los frutos, come de la vida,
tiéndete al pie del árbol, bebe el agua!,

todo se transfigura y es sagrado,
es el centro del mundo cada cuarto,
es la primera noche, el primer día,
el mundo nace cuando dos se besan,
gota de luz de entrañas transparentes
el cuarto como un fruto se entreabre
o estalla como un astro taciturno
y las leyas comidas de ratones,
las rejas de los bancos y las cárceles,
las rejas de papel, las alambradas,
los timbres y las púas y los pinchos,
el sermón monocorde de las armas,
el escorpion meloso y con bonete,
el tigre con chistera, presidente
del Club Vegetariano y la Cruz Roja,
el burro pedagogo, el cocodrilo
metido a redentor, padre de pueblos,
el Jefe, el tiburón, el arquitecto
del porvenir, el cerdo uniformado,
el hijo predilecto de la Iglesia
que se lava la negra dentadura
con el agua bendita y toma clases
de inglés y democracia, las paredes
invisibles, las máscaras podridas
que dividen al hombre de los hombres,
al hombre de sí mismo,
                              se derrumban
por un instante inmenso y vislumbramos

trap-doors, cells, oubliettes, enchanted caverns,
cages of birds, and rooms with numbers on them,
everything is transfigured, everything is in flight,
all these mouldings are clouds, and every door
opens on the sea, the field, the air; each meal
is now a celebration; sealed tight as shells,
time cannot hope, besieging them, to conquer,
there is no time here, no wall: space, space is here,
open your hand and gather these riches in,
cut all the fruits, this life is here to eat,
lie at the foot of this tree, and drink the water!

everything is transfigured and is sacred,
and each room is now the centre of the world,
tonight is the first night, today the first day,
whenever two people kiss the world is born,
a drop of light with guts of transparency
the room like a fruit splits and begins to open
or burst like a star among the silences
and all laws now rat-gnawed and eaten away,
barred windows of banks and penitentiaries,
the bars of paper, and the barbed-wire fences,
the stamps and the seals, the sharp prongs and the spurs,
the one-note sermon of the bombs and wars,
the gentle scorpion in his cap and gown,
the tiger who is the president of the Society
for the Prevention of Cruelty and the Red Cross,
the pedagogical ass, and the crocodile
set up as saviour, father of his country,
the founder, the leader, the shark, the architect
of the future of us all, the hog in uniform,
and then that one, the favourite son of the Church
who can be seen brushing his black teeth
in holy water and taking evening courses
in English and democracy, the invisible
barriers, the mad and decaying masks
that are used to separate us, man from man,
and man from his own self
                              they are thrown down
for an enormous instant and we see darkly

nuestra unidad perdida, el desamparo
que es ser hombres, la gloria que es ser hombres
y compartir el pan, el sol, la muerte,
el olvidado asombro de estar vivos;

amar es combatir, si dos se besan
el mundo cambia, encarnan los deseos,
el pensamiento encarna, brotan alas
en las espaldas del esclavo, el mundo
es real y tangible, el vino es vino,
el pan vuelve a saber, el agua es agua,
amar es combatir, es abrir puertas,
dejar de ser fantasma con un número
a perpetua cadena condenado
por un amo sin rostro;
      el mundo cambia
si dos se miran y se reconocen,
amar es desnudarse de los nombres:
'déjame ser tu puta', son palabras
de Eloísa, mas él cedió a las leyes,
la tomó por esposa y como premio
lo castraron después;
      mejor el crimen,
los amantes suicidas, el incesto
de los hermanos como dos espejos
enamorados de su semejanza,
mejor comer el pan envenenado,
el adulterio en lechos de ceniza,
los amores feroces, el delirio,
su yedra ponzoñosa, el sodomita
que lleva por clavel en la solapa
un gargajo, mejor ser lapidado
en las plazas que dar vuelta a la noria
que exprime la sustancia de la vida,
cambia la eternidad en horas huecas,
los minutos en cárceles, el tiempo
en monedas de cobre y mierda abstracta;

mejor la castidad, flor invisible
que se mece en los tallos del silencio,

our own lost unity, how vulnerable it is
to be women and men, the glory it is to be man
and share our bread and share our sun and our death,
the dark forgotten marvel of being alive;

to love is to struggle, and if two people kiss
the world is transformed, and all desires made flesh
and intellect is made flesh; great wings put forth
their shoots from the shoulders of the slave, the world
is real and to be touched and the wine is wine,
the bread can taste again, the water is water,
to love is to struggle, is to open the doors,
to stop being a fantasy with a number
condemned to the sentence of the endless chain
by a faceless master;
                        and the world is changed
when two people look at each other, recognizing
to love is to take off our clothes and our names:
'Allow me to be your whore', these are the words
of Heloise, but he gave in to the law,
he took her to be his wife, and as reward,
later, they castrated him;
                        better to have the crime,
the suicidal lovers, or the incest
between two brothers, as between two mirrors
falling in love and loving their reflections,
better to venture and eat the poisoned bread,
better adultery on beds of ashes,
the ferocious passions, and delirium,
its venomous ivy, and the sodomite
who carries for his buttonhole carnation
a gobbet of spit, better be killed by stoning
in the public square than tread the mill that grinds
out into nothing the substance of our life,
changes eternity into hollow hours,
minutes into penitentiaries, and time
into some copper pennies and abstract shit;

better take chastity, the invisible flower
swaying among the evening stalks of silence,

el difícil diamante de los santos
que filtra los deseos, sacia al tiempo,
nupcias de la quietud y el movimiento,
canta la soledad en su corola,
pétalo de cristal es cada hora,
el mundo se despoja de sus máscaras
y en su centro, vibrante transparencia,
lo que llamamos Dios, el ser sin nombre,
se contempla en la nada, el ser sin rostro
emerge de sí mismo, sol de soles,
plenitud de presencias y de nombres;

sigo mi desvarío, cuartos, calles,
camino a tientas por los corredores
del tiempo y subo y bajo sus peldaños
y sus paredes palpo y no me muevo,
vuelvo adonde empecé, busco tu rostro,
camino por las calles de mí mismo
bajo un sol sin edad, y tú a mi lado
caminas como un árbol, como un río
caminas y me hablas como un río,
creces como una espiga entre mis manos,
lates como una ardilla entre mis manos,
vuelas como mil pájaros, tu risa
me ha cubierto de espumas, tu cabeza
es un astro pequeño entre mis manos,
el mundo reverdece si sonríes
comiendo una naranja,
                              el mundo cambia
si dos, vertiginosos y enlazados,
caen sobre la yerba: el cielo baja,
los árboles ascienden, el espacio
sólo es luz y silencio, sólo espacio
abierto para el águila del ojo,
pasa la blanca tribu de las nubes,
rompe amarras el cuerpo, zarpa el alma,
perdemos nuestros nombres y flotamos
a la deriva entre el azul y el verde,
tiempo total donde no pasa nada
sino su propio transcurrir dichoso,

the difficult diamond of the saints of heaven
which filters out the desires and satiates time,
makes marriages of quietude and movement,
sings the song of solitude, her corolla,
a petal of crystal is, she sings, each hour,
the world is stripping itself of all its masks
and at its centre, vibrating, transparent,
that being we call God, the nameless being,
contemplative of itself in nothingness,
the faceless being emerging from its self,
sun of suns, fullness of presences and names;

I follow my delirium, rooms, rooms, streets,
walk groping and groping down the corridors
of time and over and under its staircases
I feel along its walls and, not advancing,
I turn to where I began, I seek your face,
walk doubtfully these dim streets of my own self
under a timeless sun and you beside me
walk with me like a tree, a river going
walk with me speaking to me like a river,
grow like a stalk of wheat among my fingers,
throb like a squirrel warm among my fingers,
flying become a thousand birds, your smiling
has covered my body with sea-foam, your head
is a nebula in small between my hands,
the world grows fresh and green while you are smiling
and eating an orange
     and the world is changed
if two people shaken by dizziness and enlaced
are fallen among the grass: the sky descending,
the trees pointing and climbing upward, and space
alone among all things is light and silence,
and pure space opens to the eagle of the eye,
and it sees pass the white tribe of the clouds,
the body's cables snap, the soul sails out,
now is the moment we lose our names, and float
along the border-line between blue and green,
the integrated time when nothing happens
but the event, belonging, communicating,

no pasa nada, callas, parpadeas
(silencio: cruzó un ángel este instante
grande como la vida de cien soles),
—no pasa nada, sólo un parpadeo?
—y el festín, el destierro, el primer crimen,
la quijada del asno, el ruido opaco
y la mirada incrédula del muerto
al caer en el llano ceniciento,
Agamenón y su mugido inmenso
y el repetido grito de Casandra
más fuerte que los gritos de las olas,
Sócrates en cadenas (el sol nace,
morir es despertar: 'Critón, un gallo
a Esculapio, ya sano de la vida'),
el chacal que diserta entre las ruinas
de Nínive, la sombra que vio Bruto
antes de la batalla, Moctezuma
en el lecho de espinas de su insomnio,
el viaje en la carreta hacia la muerte
—el viaje interminable mas contado
por Robespierre minuto tras minuto,
la mandíbula rota entre las manos—
Churruca en su barrica como un trono
escarlata, los pasos ya contados
de Lincoln al salir hacia el teatro,
el estertor de Trotski y sus quejidos
de jabalí, Madero y su mirada
que nadie contestó:—por qué me matan?,
los carajos, los ayes, los silencios
del criminal, el santo, el pobre diablo,
cementerios de frases y de anécdotas
que los perros retóricos escarban,
el delirio, el relincho, el ruido oscuro
que hacemos al morir y ese jadeo
de la vida que nace y el sonido
de huesos machacados en la riña
y la boca de espuma del profeta
y su grito y el grito del verdugo
y el grito de la víctima ...
                    son llamas

nothing happens, nothing, you become calm, blinking
(silence: an angel crosses over in this moment
enormous as the life of a hundred suns),
has nothing happened but the flickering eyelid?
—and the banquet, the exile, the first murder,
the jawbone of an ass, the city-battering sound
and the unbelieving gaze of the dead man
falling on the embers of the burning field,
and Agamemnon's lowing, immense howl,
the repetitious crying of Cassandra
a louder sound than the sound of waves crying,
and Socrates in chains (the sun is rising,
to die is to awake: 'Crito, I owe a
cock to Aesculapius, for being cured of life'),
the jackal who gives tongue among the ruins
of Nineveh, the shadow Brutus beheld
the night before the battle, Moctezuma
lying on his bed of thorns, insomnia,
the journey in the tumbril, the way to death
—the interminable journey made still longer
for Robespierre progressing inch by inch
holding his shattered jawbone in his hands—
Churruca acting as if his vat were a throne
of scarlet, and the measured steps of Lincoln
getting ready, that night, to go to theatre,
the rattle in Trotsky's throat and then his moan
as of a wild boar, Madero and his gaze
answered by nobody: why are they killing me?
the balls, the guts, the alases, silences
of the saint, the criminal, and the poor devil,
graveyards of phrases and of those anecdotes
that the old dogs of rhetoric scratch over,
delirium, whinnying, the obscure noises
which have to do with death, this panting frenzy
of life getting itself born, the scraping sounds
of bones macerated in ferocity
and the mouth of foam that is the prophet's mouth
and his cry and the cry of the torturer
and the cry of the victim ...

                         they are flames

los ojos y son llamas lo que miran,
llama la oreja y el sonido llama,
brasa los labios y tizón la lengua,
el tacto y lo que toca, el pensamiento
y lo pensado, llama el que lo piensa,
todo se quema, el universo es llama,
arde la misma nada que no es nada
sino un pensar en llamas, al fin humo:
no hay verdugo ni víctima …
                                    —y el grito
en la tarde del viernes?, y el silencio
que se cubre de signos, el silencio
que dice sin decir—no dice nada?,
—no son nada los gritos de los hombres?,
—no pasa nada cuando pasa el tiempo?

—no pasa nada, sólo un parpadeo
del sol, un movimiento apenas, nada,
no hay redención, no vuelve atrás el tiempo,
los muertos están fijos en su muerte
y no pueden morirse de otra muerte,
intocables, clavados en su gesto,
desde su soledad, desde su muerte
sin remedio nos miran sin mirarnos,
su muerte ya es la estatua de su vida,
un siempre estar ya nada para siempre,
cada minuto es nada para siempre,
un rey fantasma rige tus latidos
y tu gesto final, tu dura máscara
labra sobre tu rostro cambiante:
el monumento somos de una vida
ajena y no vivida, apenas nuestra,

—la vida, cuándo fue de veras nuestra?,
—cuándo somos de veras lo que somos?,
bien mirado no somos, nunca somos
a solas sino vértigo y vacío,
muecas en el espejo, horror y vómito,
nunca la vida es nuestra, es de los otros,
la vida no es de nadie, todos somos

the eyes are flames and those who gaze are flaming
the ear is fire and the fiery music,
live coal the lips and the tongue firebrand,
the one who touches and the one who is touching,
thinking and thought, and the thinker is a fire
and all things burn and the universe is flame,
and nothing burns like the rest, nothing which is
nothing except a thought in flames, ultimate smoke:
there is no victim and no torturer ...

                                    and the cry
that Friday afternoon? and then the silence
covering all the air with symbols, silence
which speaks without speaking, does it say nothing?
are they nothing at all, the cries of men?
does nothing happen in time but time passing?

—nothing happens, only the flickering eyelid
of the great sun, hardly a movement, nothing,
the unredeemable boundaries of time,
the dead are all pinned down by their own dying,
they cannot die again of another death,
they are untouchable, locked in their gestures,
and since their solitude and since their dying
this only can they do: stare sightless at us,
their death is simply the statue of their life,
perpetual being and nothingness without end,
for every moment is nothing without end,
a king of fantasy regulates your pulse
and your last gesture carves an impassive mask
and lays that sculpture over your mobile face:
we are the monument raised to an alien
life, a life unlived, not lively, hardly ours.

—and this our life, when was it truly ours?
and when are we truly whatever we are?
for surely we are not, we never are
anything alone but spinning and emptiness,
crazy faces made in the mirror, horror,
vomit; life is not ours, it is the others',
it is not anybody's, all of us are

la vida – pan de sol para los otros,
los otros todos que nosotros somos –
soy otro cuando soy, los actos míos
son más míos si son también de todos,
para que pueda ser he de ser otro,
salir de mí, buscarme entre los otros,
los otros que no son si yo no existo,
los otros que me dan plena existencia,
no soy, no hay yo, siempre somos nosotros,
la vida es otra, siempre allá, más lejos,
fuera de ti, de mí, siempre horizonte,
vida que nos desvive y enajena,
que nos inventa un rostro y lo desgasta,
hambre de ser, oh muerte, pan de todos,

Eloísa, Perséfona, María,
muestra tu rostro al fin para que vea
mi cara verdadera, la del otro,
mi cara de nosotros siempre todos,
cara de árbol y de panadero,
de chofer y de nube y de marino,
cara de sol y arroyo y Pedro y Pablo,
cara de solitario colectivo,
despiértame, ya nazco:
                         vida y muerte
pactan en ti, señora de la noche,
torre de claridad, reina del alba,
virgen lunar, madre del agua madre,
cuerpo del mundo, casa de la muerte,
caigo sin fin desde mi nacimiento,
caigo en mí mismo sin tocar mi fondo,
recógeme en tus ojos, junta el polvo
disperso y reconcilia mis cenizas,
ata mis huesos divididos, sopla
sobre mi ser, entiérrame en tu tierra,
tu silencio dé paz al pensamiento
contra sí mismo airado;
                      abre la mano,
señora de semillas que son días,
el día es inmortal, asciende, crece,

life—the bread of the sun for all the others,
all of those others who are us, we ourselves—
I am the other when I am myself, my acts
are more my own when they are everybody's,
because to be myself I must be other,
go out of myself, seek my self among others,
those others who are not if I do not exist,
others give me the fullness of my existence,
I am not, there is no I, We are for ever,
and life is otherwise, always *there*, farther,
beyond thee, beyond me, eternal horizon,
life that is dying for us, life that is made for
and invents us, our faces, eats them away,
the thirst for existence, death, bread of us all.

Heloise, Persephone, and Mary, thou,
turn to me then at last that you may see
my true and central face, that of the other,
my face of us all, that is always all of us,
face of the living tree and the breadman,
the driver and the thunderhead, the sailor,
the sun's face, the arroyo's, faces of Peter and Paul,
face of the individual collective,
awaken me, now I am born:
                              life and death
are reconciled in thee, lady of midnight,
tower of clarity, empress of daybreak,
moon virgin, mother of all mother liquids,
body and flesh of the world, the house of death,
I have been endlessly falling since my birth,
I fall in my own self, never touch my depth,
gather me in your eyes, at last bring together
my scattered dust, make peace among my ashes,
bind the dismemberment of my bones, and breathe
upon my being, bring me to earth in your earth,
your silence of peace to the intellectual act
against itself aroused;
                              open now your hand
lady of the seeds of life, seeds that are days,
day is an immortality, it rises, it grows,

acaba de nacer y nunca acaba,
cada día es nacer, un nacimiento
es cada amanecer y yo amanezco,
amanecemos todos, amanece
el sol cara de sol, Juan amanece
con su cara de Juan cara de todos,

puerta del ser, despiértame, amanece,
déjame ver el rostro de este día,
déjame ver el rostro de esta noche,
todo se comunica y transfigura,
arco de sangre, puente de latidos,
llévame al otro lado de esta noche,
adonde yo soy tú somos nosotros,
al reino de pronombres enlazados,

puerta del ser: abre tu ser, despierta,
aprende a ser también, labra tu cara,
trabaja tus facciones, ten un rostro
para mirar mi rostro y que te mire,
para mirar la vida hasta la muerte,
rostro de mar, de pan, de roca y fuente,
manantial que disuelve nuestros rostros
en el rostro sin nombre, el ser sin rostro,
indecible presencia de presencias ...

quiero seguir, ir más allá, y no puedo:
se despeñó el instante en otro y otro,
dormí sueños de piedra que no sueña
y al cabo de los años como piedras
oí cantar mi sangre encarcelada,
con un rumor de luz el mar cantaba,
una a una cedían las murallas,
todas las puertas se desmoronaban
y el sol entraba a saco por mi frente,
despegaba mis párpados cerrados,
desprendía mi ser de su envoltura,
me arrancaba de mí, me separaba
de mi bruto dormir siglos de piedra
y su magia de espejos revivía

is done with being born and never is done,
every day is a birth, and every daybreak
another birthplace and I am the break of day,
we all dawn on the day, the sun dawns
and daybreak is the face of the sun, John
is the break of day with John's face, face of all,

gate of our being, awaken me, bring dawn,
grant that I see the face of the living day,
grant that I see the face of this live night,
everything speaks now, everything is transformed,
O arch of blood, bridge of our pulse beating,
carry me through to the far side of this night,
the place where I am You, equals Ourselves,
kingdom of persons and pronouns intertwined,

gateway of being: open your being, awaken,
learn then to be, begin to carve your face,
develop your elements, and keep your vision
keen to look at my face, as I at yours,
keen to look full at life right through to death,
faces of sea, of bread, of rock, of fountain,
the spring of origin which will dissolve our faces
in the nameless face, existence without face
the inexpressible presence of presences ...

I want to go on, to go beyond; I cannot;
the moment scatters itself in many things,
I have slept the dreams of the stone that never dreams
and deep among the dreams of years like stones
have heard the singing of my imprisoned blood,
with a premonition of light the sea sang,
and one by one the barriers give way,
all of the gates have fallen to decay,
the sun has forced an entrance through my forehead,
has opened my eyelids at last that were kept closed,
unfastened my being of its swaddling clothes,
has rooted me out of my self, and separated
me from my animal sleep centuries of stone
and the magic of reflections resurrects

33

un sauce de cristal, un chopo de agua,
un alto surtidor que el viento arquea,
un árbol bien plantado mas danzante,
un caminar de río que se curva,
avanza, retrocede, da un rodeo
y llega siempre:

willow of crystal, a poplar of water,
a pillar of fountain by the wind drawn over,
tree that is firmly rooted and that dances,
turning course of a river that goes curving,
advances and retreats, goes roundabout,
arriving for ever:

[M.R.]

From
Salamandra
(1958–61)

Solo a dos voces

En ninguna otra lengua occidental son tantas las palabras fantasmas ...

J. Corominas, Diccionario Crítico-Etimológico de la Lengua Castellana

Si decir No
Al mundo al presente
Hoy (solsticio de invierno)
No es decir
        Si
Decir es solsticio de invierno
Hoy en el mundo
            No
Es decir
     Si
Decir mundo presente
No es decir
        Qué es
Mundo Solsticio Invierno?
Qué es decir?
          (Desde hace horas
Oigo caer, en el patio negro,
Una gota de agua.
Ella cae y yo escribo.)

Solsticio de invierno:
Sol parado
          Mundo errante
Sol desterrado
            Fijeza al rojo blanco
La tierra blanca negra
Dormida
Sobre sí misma echada
Es una piedra caída
Ánima en pena
          El mundo
Peña de pena

Solo for two voices

In no other occidental language are there so many ghost words ...

J. Corominas, Diccionario Crítico-Etimológico
de la Lengua Castellana

If saying No
To the world to the present
This day (the winter solstice)
Is not saying
                    Yes if
Saying is the winter solstice
Today in the world
                         It is not
Saying
         Yes if
Saying the world the present
Is not saying
                    What is
Winter Solstice World?
What is saying?
                    (For hours now
I've heard falling, in the black patio,
A drop of water.
It falls and I write.)

Winter solstice:
Sun stopped
                  World wandering
Sun in exile
                  Fixity at white heat
The black white earth
Asleep
Flung on itself
Is a fallen stone
Soul in purgatory
                       The world
Purgatorial stone

El alma
Peña entrañas de piedra
(Cae la gota invisible
Sobre el cemento húmedo.
Cae también en mi cuarto.
A la mitad del pensamiento
Me quedo, como el sol,
Parado
En la mitad de mí,
Separado.)

Mundo mondo,
Sonaja de semillas semánticas:
Vírgenes móndigas
        (Mundicas,
Las que llevan el mundum
El día de la procesión),
Muchachas cereales
Ofrendan a Ceres panes y ceras;
Muchachas trigueñas,
Entre el pecho y los ojos
Alzan la monda,
Pascua de Resurrección:
Señora del Prado,
        Sobre tu cabeza,
Como una corona cándida,
La canasta del pan.

Incandescencias del candeal,
Muchachas, cestas de panes,
Pan de centeno y pan de cebada,
Pan de abejas, pan de flor,
Altar vivo los pechos,
Sobre mesa de tierra vasos de sol:
Como y bebo, hombre soy.
(Sonaja de simientes, poema:
Enterrar la palabra,
El grano de fuego,
En el cuerpo de Ceres

The soul
Stone with stony heart
(The drop falls unseen
On the wet cement.
It falls too in my room.
Midway in thought
I stay, like the sun,
Stopped
Midway in myself,
Separated.)

Mundo mondo, clean world,
Rattle of semantic seeds:
Virgin *móndigas*
                    (*Mundicas,*
Those that carry the mundum
The day the procession is held),
Girls of the grain
Offer to Ceres loaves and beeswax;
Girls like tawny wheat,
Between their breast and their eyes
Lift the offering,
At Easter-tide:
Our Lady of the Meadow,
                              On your head,
As if crowned with candour,
The basket of bread.

Incandescences of white bread,
Girls, baskets of loaves,
Rye bread and barley bread,
Bread with a bee design, the fine white bread,
The breasts a living altar,
Goblets of sun on the table of earth:
I eat and I drink, am a man.
(Rattle of seeds, poem:
To bury the word in earth,
The kernel of fire,
In the body of Ceres

Tres veces arado;
Enterrarla en el patio,
Horadar el cemento
Con la gota tenaz,
Con la gota de tinta.
Para la diosa negra,
Piedra dormida en la nieve,
Dibujar un caballo de agua,
Dibujar en la página
Un caballo de yerba ...)

Hoy es solsticio de invierno:
Canta el gallo
         El sol despierta.
Voces y risas, baile y panderos.
Sobre el suelo entumido
Rumor de faldas de muchachas
Como el viento corriendo entre espadañas,
Como el agua que brota de la peña.
Muchachas,
        Cántaros penantes,
El agua se derrama,
El vino se derrama,
El fuego se derrama,
Penetra las entrañas,
La piedra se despierta:
Lleva un sol en el vientre.
Como el pan en el horno,
El hijo de la piedra incandescente
Es el hijo de nadie.
(A solas con el diccionario
Agito el ramo seco,
Palabras, muchachas, semillas,
Sonido de guijarros
Sobre la tierra negra y blanca,
Inanimada.
En el aire frío del patio
Se dispersan las vírgenes.
Humedad y cemento.)

Three times ploughed;
To bury it in the patio,
Drill through the cement
With the persistent drop,
With the drop of ink.
For the dark goddess,
Stone asleep in the snow,
To sketch a horse of water,
To scrawl on the page
A horse of grass ...)

Today is the winter solstice:
The rooster crows
                              The sun awakens.
Voices and laughter, dancing and tambourines.
Over the numb earth
Rustle of skirts of girls
Like the wind as it runs through the rushes,
Like the water that bursts from the rock.
Girls,
        Jars, slender-throated,
The water runs over,
The wine runs over,
The fire runs over,
Goes deep into the body,
The stone awakens:
Bears a sun in its womb.
Like a loaf in the oven,
The child of the white-hot stone,
Is the child of no one.
(Alone with the dictionary
I shake the dry branch,
Words, girls, seeds,
The rattle of pebbles
On the earth black and white,
Without life.
In the cold air of the patio
The virgins scatter.
Wetness and cement.)

El mundo
No es tortas y pan pintado.
El diccionario
Es un mundo no dicho:
De solsticio (de invierno)
A pascua (de resurrección),
En dirección inversa
A las agujas del cuadrante,
Hay: 'sofisma, símil, selacio, salmo,
Rupestre, rosca, ripio, réprobo,
Rana, Quito, quejido,
Pulque, ponzoña, picotín, peluca ... '
Desandar el camino,
Volver a la primera letra
En dirección inversa
Al sol,
          Hacia la piedra:
Simiente,
          Gota de energía,
Joya verde
Entre los pechos negros de la diosa.
(Escribo contra la corriente,
Contra la aguja hipnotizada
Y los sofismas del cuadrante:
Como la sombra, la aguja
Sigue al sol,
               Un sol sin cuerpo,
Sombra de sol,
               Siempre futuro;
Como un perro, la aguja
Tras los pasos del sol,
                    Sol ido,
Desvanecido, sol de sombra.)

No el movimiento del círculo,
Maestro de espejismos:
                         La quietud
En el centro del movimiento.
No predecir: decir.
Mundo suspendido en la sombra,

The world
Is not all cakes and fancy bread.
The dictionary is a world not spoken:
From solstice (the winter one)
To Easter (the resurrection)
In a direction contrary
To that of the sundial-marker,
Occur: 'spiral, sophism, similar, selachian,
Rocky, refuse, reprobate, quartern,
Querulous, Quito, pulque, psalm,
Pollywog, poison, periwig ... '
Retracing the road,
Going back to the first letter
In a direction contrary
To that of the sun,
                    Towards the stone:
Seed,
      Drop of energy,
Green jewel
Between the dark breasts of the goddess.
(I write against the current,
Against the mesmerized marker
And the plausible lies of the sundial:
Like the shadow, the marker
Follows the sun,
                    A sun without body,
Shade of a sun,
                    For ever future;
Like a dog, the marker
Hard on the heels of the sun,
                            A sun gone,
Vanished, sun of shade.)

Not the movement of the circle,
Master of mirages:
                    The quietude
At the centre of the movement.
Not to foretell: to tell.
World suspended in the shadow,

Mundo mondo, pulido como hueso,
Decir es mondadura,
Poda del árbol de los muertos.
Decir es penitencia de palabras,
La zona negra y blanca,
El húmedo cemento, el patio,
El no saber qué digo
Entre la ausencia y la presencia
De este mundo, echado
Sobre su propio abandono,
Caído como gota de tinta.
(La letra no reposa en la página:
Memoria la levanta,
Monumento de viento.
Y quién recuerda a la memoria,
Quién la levanta, dónde se implanta?
Frente de claridad, alumbramiento,
La memoria es raíz en la tiniebla.)

Come tiniebla,
               Come olvido:
No lo que dices, lo que olvidas,
Es lo que dices:
               Hoy es solsticio de invierno
En el mundo
               Hoy estás separado
En el mundo
               Hoy es el mundo
Anima en pena en el mundo.

Clean world, clean as bone,
Saying is a paring away,
A pruning of the tree of the dead.
Saying is a penance of words,
The black-and-white zone,
The wet cement, the patio,
The not knowing what I say
Between the absence and the presence
Of this world, flung
On its own abandonment,
Fallen like a drop of ink.
(The letter does not lie still on the page:
Memory arouses it,
Monument of wind.
And who is the reminder of memory,
Who raises it, where is it planted?
Brow of brightness, the lightening womb,
Memory is a root in the dark.)

Feed on the dark,
                Feed on forgetfulness:
Not what you say, what you forget,
Is what you say:
                Today is the winter solstice
In the world
                Today you are separated
In the world
                Today is the world
Purgatorial soul in the world.

[J.F.N.]

47

Madrugada

Rápidas manos frías
Retiran una a una
Las vendas de la sombra
Abro los ojos
          Todavía
Estoy vivo
        En el centro
De una herida todavía fresca

Dawn

Cold rapid hands
Draw back one by one
The bandages of dark
I open my eyes
               Still
I am living
          At the centre
Of a wound still fresh

[C.T.]

Aquí

Mis pasos en esta calle
Resuenan
        En otra calle
Donde
     Oigo mis pasos
Pasar en esta calle
Donde

Sólo es real la niebla

Here

My steps along this street
Resound
          In another street
In which
          I hear my steps
Passing along this street
In which

Only the mist is real

[C.T.]

Oráculo

Los labios fríos de la noche
Dicen una palabra
Columna de pena
Piedra y no palabra
Sombra y no piedra
Pensamiento de humo
Agua real para mis labios de humo
Palabra de verdad
Razón de mis errores
Si es muerte sólo por ella vivo
Si es soledad hablo por ella
Es la memoria y no recuerdo nada
No sé lo que dice y a ella me fío
Como saberse vivo
Como olvidar que lo sabemos
Tiempo que entreabre los párpados
Y se deja mirar y nos mira

Oracle

The cold lips of the night
Utter a word
Column of grief
No word but stone
No stone but shadow
Vaporous thought
Through my vaporous lips real water
Word of truth
Reason behind my errors
If it is death only through that do I live
If it is solitude I speak in serving it
It is memory and I remember nothing
I do not know what it says and I trust myself to it
How to know oneself living
How to forget one's knowing
Time that half-opens the eyelids
And sees us, letting itself be seen

[C.T.]

Amistad

Es la hora esperada
Sobre la mesa cae
Interminablemente
La cabellera de la lámpara
La noche vuelve inmensa la ventana
No hay nadie
La presencia sin nombre me rodea

Friendship

It is the awaited hour
Over the table falls
Interminably
The lamp's spread hair
Night turns the window to immensity
There is no one here
Presence without name surrounds me

[C.T.]

Certeza

Si es real la luz blanca
De esta lámpara, real
La mano que escribe, son reales
Los ojos que miran lo escrito?

De una palabra a la otra
Lo que digo se desvanece.
Yo sé que estoy vivo
Entre dos paréntesis.

Certainty

If it is real the white
Light from this lamp, real
The writing hand, are they
Real, the eyes looking at what I write?

From one word to the other
What I say vanishes.
I know that I am alive
Between two parentheses.

[C.T.]

Paisaje

Peña y precipicio,
Más tiempo que piedra,
Materia sin tiempo.

Por sus cicatrices
Sin moverse cae
Perpetua agua virgen.

Reposa lo inmenso
Piedra sobre piedra,
Piedras sobre aire.

Se despliega el mundo
Tal cual es, inmóvil
Sol en el abismo.

Balanza del vértigo:
Las rocas no pesan
Más que nuestras sombras.

Landscape

Rock and precipice,
More time than stone, this
Timeless matter.

Through its cicatrices
Falls without moving
Perpetual virgin water.

Immensity reposes here
Rock on rock,
Rocks over air.

The world's manifest
As it is: a sun
Immobile, in the abyss.

Scale of vertigo:
The crags weigh
No more than our shadows.

[C.T.]

Cosante

Con la lengua cortada
Y los ojos abiertos
El ruiseñor en la muralla

Ojos de pena acumulada
Y plumaje de sangre
El ruiseñor en la muralla

Plumas de sangre y breve llamarada
Agua recién nacida en la garganta
El ruiseñor en la muralla

Agua que corre enamorada
Agua con alas
El ruiseñor en la muralla

Entre las piedras negras la voz blanca
Del agua enamorada
El ruiseñor en la muralla

Con la lengua cortada canta
Sangre sobre la piedra
El ruiseñor en la muralla

Cosante

With a slit tongue
And open eyes
The nightingale on the ramparts

Eyes of stored-up pain
And feathers of blood
The nightingale on the ramparts

Feathers of blood and brief dazzle
Fresh water given birth in the throat
The nightingale on the ramparts

Water that runs stricken with love
Water with wings
The nightingale on the ramparts

Among black stones the white voice
Of love-struck water
The nightingale on the ramparts

Singing with slit tongue
Blood on the stone
The nightingale on the ramparts

[D.L.]

Palpar

Mis manos
Abren las cortinas de tu ser
Te visten con otra desnudez
Descubren los cuerpos de tu cuerpo
Mis manos
Inventan otro cuerpo a tu cuerpo

Touch

My hands
Open the curtains of your being
Clothe you in a further nudity
Uncover the bodies of your body
My hands
Invent another body for your body

[C.T.]

Duración

I

Negro el cielo
                Amarilla la tierra
El gallo desgarra la noche
El agua se levanta y pregunta la hora
El viento se levanta y pregunta por ti
Pasa un caballo blanco

II

Como el bosque en su lecho de hojas
Tú duermes en tu lecho de lluvia
Tú cantas en tu lecho de viento
Tú besas en tu lecho de chispas

III

Olor vehemencia numerosa
Cuerpo de muchas manos
Sobre un tallo invisible
Una sola blancura

IV

Habla escucha respóndeme
Lo que dice el trueno
Lo comprende el bosque

V

Entro por tus ojos
Sales por mi boca
Duermes en mi sangre
Despierto en tu frente

Duration

I

Sky black
        Yellow earth
The rooster tears the night apart
The water wakes and asks what time it is
The wind wakes and asks for you
A white horse goes by

II

As the forest in its bed of leaves
You sleep in your bed of rain
You sing in your bed of wind
You kiss in your bed of sparks

III

Multiple vehement odour
Many-handed body
On an invisible stem a single
Whiteness

IV

Speak listen answer me
What the thunder-clap
Says, the woods
Understand

V

I enter by your eyes
You come forth by my mouth
You sleep in my blood
I waken in your head

VI

Te hablaré un lenguaje de piedra
(Respondes con un monosílabo verde)
Te hablaré un lenguaje de nieve
(Respondes con un abanico de abejas)
Te hablaré un lenguaje de agua
(Respondes con una canoa de relámpagos)
Te hablaré un lenguaje de sangre
(Respondes con una torre de pájaros)

VI

I will speak to you in stone-language
(Answer with a green syllable)
I will speak to you in snow-language
(Answer with a fan of bees)
I will speak to you in water-language
(Answer with a canoe of lightning)
I will speak to you in blood-language
(Answer with a tower of birds)

[D.L.]

Ustica

Los sucesivos soles del verano,
La sucesión del sol y sus veranos,
Todos los soles,
El solo, el sol de soles,
Hechos ya hueso terco y leonado,
Cerrazón de materia enfriada.

Puño de piedra,
Piña de lava,
Osario,
No tierra,
Isla tampoco,
Peña despeñada,
Duro durazno,
Gota de sol petrificada.

Por las noches se oye
El respirar de las cisternas,
El jadeo del agua dulce
Turbada por el mar.
La hora es alta y rayada de verde.
El cuerpo oscuro del vino
En las jarras dormido
Es un sol más negro y fresco.

Aquí la rosa de las profundidades
Es un candelabro de venas rosadas
Encendido en el fondo del mar.
En tierra, el sol lo apaga,
Pálido encaje calcáreo
Como el deseo labrado por la muerte.

Ustica

The successive suns of summer,
The succession of the sun and of its summers,
All the suns,
The sole, the sol of sols
Now become
Obstinate and tawny bone,
Darkness-before-the-storm
Of matter cooled.

Fist of stone,
Pine-cone of lava,
Ossuary,
Not earth
Nor island either,
Rock off a rock-face,
Hard peach,
Sun-drop petrified.

Through the nights one hears
The breathing of cisterns,
The panting of fresh water
Troubled by the sea.
The hour is late and the light, greening.
The obscure body of the wine
Asleep in jars
Is a darker and cooler sun.

Here the roses of the depths
Is a candelabrum of pinkish veins
Kindled on the sea-bed.
Ashore, the sun extinguishes it,
Pale, chalky lace
As if desire were worked by death.

Rocas color de azufre,
Altas piedras adustas.
Tú estás a mi costado.
Tus pensamientos son negros y dorados.
Si alargase la mano
Cortaría un racimo de verdades intactas.
Abajo, entre peñas centelleantes,
Va y viene el mar lleno de brazos.
Vértigos. La luz se precipita.
Yo te miré a la cara,
Yo me asomé al abismo:
Mortalidad es transparencia.

Osario, paraíso:
Nuestras raíces anudadas
En el sexo, en la boca deshecha
De la Madre enterrada.
Jardín de árboles incestuosos
Sobre la tierra de los muertos.

Cliffs the colour of sulphur,
High austere stones.
You are beside me.
Your thoughts are black and golden.
To extend a hand
Is to gather a cluster of truths intact.
Below, between sparkling rocks
Goes and comes
A sea full of arms.
Vertigoes. The light hurls itself headlong.
I looked you in the face,
I saw into the abyss:
Mortality is transparency.

Ossuary: paradise:
Our roots, knotted
In sex, in the undone mouth
Of the buried Mother.
Incestuous trees
That maintain
A garden on the dead's domain.

[C.T.]

Salamandra

Salamandra (negra
Armadura viste el fuego)
Calorífero de combustión lenta
(Entre las fauces
               O mármol o ladrillo
De la chimenea
              Tortuga estática
O agazapado guerrero japonés
Y una u otro
          El martirio es reposo
Impasible en la tortura)
                Salamandra
Nombre antiguo del fuego (y antídoto
Antiguo contra el fuego) y desollada
Planta que marcha sobre brasas
(Amianto amante amianto)
Salamandra
En la ciudad abstracta
Entre las geometrías vertiginosas
Formidables
Quimeras levantadas por el cálculo
Y por la sed multiplicadas
Al flanco del cristal la piedra el aluminio
Amapola súbita
                Salamandra
Garra amarilla (Roja escritura
En la pared de sal) garra de sol
Sobre el montón de huesos
Salamandra
           Estrella caída
En el sinfín del ópalo sangriento
Sepultada

Salamander

Salamander
        (the fire wears
        black armour)
a slow-burning stove
                (between the jaws
                  marble or brick
                of the chimney it is
                an ecstatic tortoise, a crouched
                Japanese warrior:
whatever it is, martyrdom
is repose
impassive under torture)
Salamander
ancient name of fire
                (and ancient
                antidote to fire)
Flayed sole of the foot walking
on hot coals
Amianthus *amante* amianthus
Salamander
in the abstract city between
dizzy geometries
formidable chimeras appear
raised up by calculus
multiplied by thirst
            crystal flanks
            rock
            aluminium
Sudden poppy
  Salamander
Yellow claw (a scrawl
of red letters on a
wall of salt)

Bajo los párpados del sílex
Niña perdida
En el túnel del ónix
En los círculos del basalto
Enterrada semilla
                    Grano de energía
Dormida en la medula del granito
Salamandra niña dinamitera
En el pecho azul y negro del hierro
Estallas como un sol
Te abres como una herida
Hablas como una fuente
Salamandra
            Espiga
Hija del fuego
Espíritu del fuego
Condensación de la sangre
Sublimación de la sangre
Evaporación de la sangre
Salamandra de aire
La roca es llama
                La llama es humo
Vapor rojo
            Recta plegaria
Alta palabra de alabanza
Exclamación Corona de incendio
En la testa del himno
Reina escarlata
(Y muchacha de medias moradas
Corriendo despeinada por el bosque)
Salamandra
Animal taciturno
Negro paño de lágrimas de azufre
(Un húmedo verano
Entre las baldosas desunidas
De un patio petrificado por la luna
Oí vibrar tu cola cilíndrica)
Salamandra caucásica
(En la espalda cenicienta de la peña
Aparece y desaparece

74

Claw of sunlight
on a heap of bones
Salamander
fallen star
in the endlessness of bloodstained opal
ensepulchred
beneath eyelids of quartz
lost girl
in tunnels of onyx
in the circles of basalt
buried seed
grain of energy
in the marrow of granite
Salamander, you who lay dynamite in iron's
black and blue breast
you explode like a sun
you open yourself like a wound
you speak
as a fountain speaks
Salamander
Blade of wheat
daughter of fire
spirit of fire
Condensation of blood
sublimation of blood
Salamander of air
the rock is flame
the flame is smoke
red vapour
straight–rising prayer
lofty word of praise
exclamation
crown
of fire on the head of the psalm
scarlet queen
(and girl with purple stockings
running dishevelled through the woods)
Salamander, you are
silent, the
black consoler of sulphur tears

Breve y negra lengüeta
Moteada de azafrán)
                    Salamandra
Bicho negro y brillante
Escalofrío del musgo
Devorador de insectos
Heraldo diminuto del chubasco
Y familiar de la centella
(*Fecundación interna*
Reproducción ovípara
Las crías viven en el agua
Ya adultas nadan con torpeza)
Salamandra
Puente colgante entre las eras
Puente de sangre fría
Eje del movimiento
(*Los cambios de la alpina*
La especie más esbelta
Se cumplen en el claustro de la madre
Entre los huevecillos se logran dos apenas
Y hasta el alumbramiento
Medran los embriones en un caldo nutricio
La masa fraternal de huevos abortados)
La salamandra española
Montañesa negra y roja
(No late el sol clavado en la mitad del cielo
No respira
No comienza la vida sin la sangre
Sin la brasa del sacrificio
No se mueve la rueda de los días
Xólotl se niega a consumirse
Se escondió en el maíz pero lo hallaron
Se escondió en el maguey pero lo hallaron
Cayó en el agua y fue el pez axólotl
El dos-seres
                    Y 'luego lo mataron'
Comenzó el movimiento anduvo el mundo
La procesión de fechas y de nombres
Xólotl el perro guía del infierno
El que desenterró los huesos de los padres

One wet summer I heard
the vibration of your
cylindrical tail
between loose tiles of a
dead-calm moonlit patio
Caucasian salamander
(in the rock's
cindery shoulder appears
and disappears
a brief black tongue
flecked with saffron)
Black and brilliant creature
the moss
quivers
you devour
insects
diminutive herald of the rain-shower
familiar spirit of the lightning
(*Internal fecundation*
Oviparous reproduction
The young live in the water
Once adult they swim sluggishly)
Salamander
hanging bridge between eras
bridge of cold blood
axis of movement
(*The changes in the alpine species*
the most slender of all
take place in the mother's womb
Of all the tiny eggs no more than two mature
and until they hatch
the embryos are nourished on a broth
composed of the doughy mass of their aborted brother-eggs)
The Spanish Salamander
black and red mountaineer
(The sun nailed to the sky's centre does not throb
does not breathe
Life does not commence without blood
Without the embers of sacrifice
the wheel of days does not revolve

El que coció los huesos en la olla
El que encendió la lumbre de los años
El hacedor de hombres
Xólotl el penitente
El ojo reventado que llora por nosotros
Xólotl la larva de la mariposa
El doble de la Estrella
El caracol marino
La otra cara del Señor de la Aurora
Xólotl el ajolote)
                Salamandra
Dardo solar
             Lámpara de la luna
Columna del mediodía
Nombre de mujer
Balanza de la noche
(El infinito peso de la luz
Un adarme de sombra en tus pestañas)
Salamandra
           Llama negra
Heliotropo
         Sol tú misma
Y luna siempre en torno de ti misma
Granada que se abre cada noche
Astro fijo en la frente del cielo
Y latido del mar y luz ya quieta
Mente sobre el vaivén del mar abierta
(*Salamandria*
Saurio de unos ocho centímetros
Vive en las grietas y es color de polvo)
Salamandra de tierra y de agua
Piedra verde en la boca de los muertos
Piedra de encarnación
Piedra de lumbre
Sudor de la tierra
Sal llameante y quemante
Sal de la destrucción
Y máscara de cal que consume los rostros
Salamandra de aire y de fuego
Avispero de soles

Xólotl refuses to consume himself
He hid himself in the corn but they found him
he hid himself in the maguey but they found him
he fell into the water and became the fish axólotl
the Double-Being
                    'and then they killed him'
Movement began, the world was set in motion
the procession of dates and names
Xólotl the dog, guide to Hell
he who dug up the bones of the fathers
he who cooked the bones in a pot
he who lit the fire of the years
the Maker of Men
Xólotl the penitent
the burst eye that weeps for us
Xólotl
            larva of the butterfly
            double of the Star
            Sea-shell
            other face of the Lord of Dawn
Xólotl the axólotl)
                        Salamander
solar arrow
lamp of the moon
column of noonday
name of woman
scales of night
                the infinite weight of light
                a half-drachm on your eyelashes
salamander
back flame
sunflower
            you yourself the sun
            the moon
            turning for ever around you
pomegranate that bursts itself open each night
fixed star on the brow of the sky
and beat of the sea and the stilled light
open mind above the
                        to-and-fro of the sea

Roja palabra del principio

La salamandra es un lagarto
Su lengua termina en un dardo
Su cola termina en un dardo
Es inasible Es indecible
Reposa sobre brasas
Reina sobre tizones
Si en la llama se esculpe
Su monumento incendia
El fuego es su pasión es su *paciencia*

Salamadre   Aguamadre

The star-lizard, salamandria
saurian scarcely eight centimetres long
lives in crevices and is the colour of dust
Salamander of earth and water
green stone in the mouth of the dead
stone of incarnation
stone of fire
sweat of the earth
salt flaming and scorching
salt of destruction and
mask of lime that consumes the face
Salamander of air and fire
                    Wasp's nest of suns
                    red word of beginning

The salamander
a lizard
her tongue ends in a dart
her tail ends in a dart
she rests upon hot coals
queens it over firebrands
If she carries herself in the flame
she burns her monument
Fire is her passion, her *patience*

Salamander   Salamater

[D.L.]

From
Ladera Este
(1962–8)

El balcón

Quieta
En mitad de la noche
No a la deriva de los siglos
No tendida
       Clavada
Como idea fija
En el centro de la incandescencia
Delhi
     Dos sílabas altas
Rodeadas de arena e insomnio
En voz baja las digo
          Nada se mueve
Y sin embargo
        Crece
La oleada silenciosa se dilata
Es el verano que se derrama
Oigo la vibración del cielo bajo
Sobre los llanos en letargo
Masas enormes cónclaves obscenos
Nubes llenas de insectos
Aplastan
       Indecisos bultos enanos
(Mañana tendrán nombre
Erguidos serán casas
Mañana serán árboles)
Nada se mueve
        Y sin embargo
La hora es más grande
          Yo más solo
Clavado
      En el centro del torbellino
Si extiendo la mano

The balcony

Quiet
In the middle of the night
Not drifting with the centuries
Not sprawling
        Nailed
Like an idée fixe
In the centre of incandescence
Delhi
     Two tall syllables
Ringed by sand and insomnia
I speak them in a hushed voice
                Nothing moves
And nevertheless
             The silent tide
Grows spreads out
It is summer overflowing
I hear the vibration of the low sky
Over the lethargic plains
Enormous masses obscene congregations
Clouds full of insects
Flatten
       Indecisive dwarf bundles
(Tomorrow they will have names
They will stand up and be houses
Tomorrow they will be trees)
Nothing moves
          And nevertheless
The hour is larger
            I'm more alone
Nailed
     In the middle of the whirlwind
If I stretch out my hand

Un cuerpo fofo el aire
Un ser promiscuo sin cara
Acodado al balcón
                    Veo
(*No te apoyes,*
Si estás solo, contra la balaustrada,
Dice el poeta chino)
No es la altura ni la noche y su luna
No son los infinitos a la vista
Es la memoria y sus vértigos
Esto que veo
                    Esto que gira
Son las acechanzas las trampas
Detrás no hay nada
Son las fechas y sus remolinos
(Trono de hueso
                    Trono del mediodía
Aquella isla
                    En su cantil leonado
Por un instante vi la vida verdadera
Tenía la cara de la muerte
Eran el mismo rostro
                    Disuelto
En el mismo mar centelleante)
Lo que viviste hoy te desvive
No estás allá
                    Aquí
Estoy aquí
                    En mi comienzo
No me reniego
                    Me sustento
Acodado al balcón
                    Veo
Nubarrones y un pedazo de luna
Lo que está aquí visible
Casas gente
                    Lo real presente
Vencido por la hora
                    Lo que está allá
Invisible

86

The air is a body like a sponge
A faceless ambiguous being
Elbows leaning on the balcony
                              I see
(*Never lean*
On the balustrade if you are alone
Says the Chinese poet)
It is not the height nor the night and its moon
The infinities are not in view
It is the memory and its vertigoes
What I see
              That it spins
These are the traps the snares
There is nothing behind
These are the days and their whirlwinds
(Throne of bone
                 Throne of noon
That island
In its lion-coloured ledges
I saw for an instant what life is
It had the face of death
They were the same face
                              Dissolved
In the same flashing sea)
What you lived you unlive today
You are not there
                   Here
I am here
          It is my beginning
I do not disown myself
                        I sustain myself
Elbows leaning on the balcony
                              I see
Big clouds a bit of moon
What is visible here
Houses people
             The real present
Defeated by the hour
                     What is there
Invisible

                    Mi horizonte
Si es un comienzo este comienzo
No principia conmigo
                    Con él comienzo
En él me perpetúo
                    Acodado al balcón
Veo
    Esta lejanía tan próxima
No se como nombrarla
Aunque la toco con el pensamiento
La noche que se va a pique
La ciudad como un monte caído
Blancas luces azules amarillas
Faros súbitos paredes de infamia
Y los racimos terribles
Las piñas de hombres y bestias por el suelo
Y la maraña de sus sueños enlazados
Vieja Delhi fétida Delhi
Callejas y plazuelas y mezquitas
Como un cuerpo acuchillado
Como un jardín enterrado
Desde hace siglos llueve polvo
Tu manto son las tolvaneras
Tu almohada un ladrillo roto
En una hoja de higuera
Comes las sobras de tus dioses
Tus templos son burdeles de incurables
Estás cubierta de hormigas
Corral desamparado
                    Mausoleo desmoronado
Estás desnuda
                Como un cadáver profanado
Te arrancaron joyas y mortaja
Estabas cubierta de poemas
Todo tu cuerpo era escritura
Acuérdate
            Recobra la palabra
Eres hermosa
                Sabes hablar cantar bailar
Delhi

My horizon
If this beginning is a beginning
It does not begin with me
I begin with it
                    I perpetuate myself in it
Elbows leaning on the balcony
                              I see
This distance that is so near
I do not know how to name it
Although I touch it with my thoughts
The night that is capsizing
The city like a fallen mountain
White blue yellow
Sudden head-lights walls of infamy
And the terrible clusters
The huddles of men and animals on the ground
And the tangle of their intertwined dreams
Old Delhi fetid Delhi
Alleys and little squares and mosques
Like a stabbed body
Like a buried garden
Dust has rained down for centuries
Your veil is the clouds of dust
Your pillow is a broken brick
You eat from a fig-leaf
The scraps left by your gods
Your temples are brothels for incurables
You are covered with ants
Abandoned yard
                    Ruined mausoleum
You are naked
                    Like a violated corpse
They snatched away your gems and grave-clothes
You were covered with poems
Your whole body was writing
Remember
                    Recover the word
You are beautiful
You know how to sing speak dance
Delhi

Dos torres
Plantadas en el llano
                    Dos sílabas altas
Yo las digo en voz baja
Acodado al balcón
                    Clavado
No en el suelo
                    En su vértigo
En el centro de la incandescencia
Estuve allá
            No sé adonde
Estoy aquí
            No sé es donde
No la tierra
            El tiempo
En sus manos vacías me sostiene
Noche y luna
                    Movimientos de nubes
Temblor de árboles
                    Estupor del espacio
Infinito y violencia en el aire
Polvo iracundo que despierta
Encienden luces en el puerto aéreo
Rumor de cantos por el Fuerte Rojo
Lejanías
Pasos de un peregrino son errante
Sobre este frágil puente de palabras
La hora me levanta
Hambre de encarnación padece el tiempo
Más allá de mi mismo
En algún lado aguardo mi llegada

Two towers
Planted on the plain
Two tall syllables
I speak them in a hushed voice
Elbows leaning on the balcony
                              Nailed
Not in the ground
                    In its vertigo
In the centre of the incandescence
I was there
                I do not know is where
I am here
                I do not know where
Not the earth
              But time
Sustains me in its empty hands
Night and moon
                    Movements of clouds
Trees trembling
                    Stupor of space
Infinity and violence in the air
Wrathful dust awakening
Lights are turned on at the airport
Murmur of singing from the Red Fort
Distances
Measures of a strange and wandering song
Over this fragile bridge of words
The hour lifts me up
Time suffers from a hunger for incarnation
Somewhere beyond myself
I await my arrival

[L.K.]

El mausoleo de Humayun

Al debate de las avispas
La dialéctica de los monos
Gorjeos de las estadísticas
Opone
          (Alta llama rosa
Hecha de piedra y aire y pájaros
Tiempo en reposo sobre el agua)

La arquitectura del silencio

The mausoleum of Humayun

To the debate of wasps
The dialectic of monkeys
Twitterings of statistics
It opposes
            (High flame of rose
Formed out of stone and air and birds
Time in repose above the water)

Silence's architecture

[C.T.]

Pueblo

Las piedras son tiempo
                    El viento
Siglos de viento
                    Los árboles son tiempo
Las gentes son piedra
                    El viento
Vuelve sobre si mismo y se entierra
En el día de piedra

No hay agua pero brillan los ojos

Village

The stones are time
     The wind
Centuries of wind
     The trees are time
The people are stone
     The wind
Turns upon itself and sinks
Into the stone day

There is no water here for all the lustre of its eyes

           [C.T.]

El día en Udaipur

Blanco el palacio,
Blanco en el lago negro.
Lingam y yoni.

    Como la diosa al dios
    Tú me rodeas, noche.

Fresca terraza.
Eres inmensa, inmensa
A la medida.

    Estrellas inhumanas.
    Pero la hora es nuestra.

Caigo y me elevo,
Ardo y me anego. Sólo
Tienes un cuerpo?

    Pájaros sobre el agua,
    Alba sobre los párpados.

Ensimismados,
Altos como la muerte,
Brotan los mármoles.

    Encallan los palacios?
    Blancura a la deriva.

Mujeres, niños
Por los caminos. Frutas
Desparramadas.

The day in Udaipur

White palace,
White on the black lake.
Lingam and yoni.

> As the goddess the god,
> You surround me, night.

The cool terrace.
You are immense, immense
Made to measure.

> Inhuman stars.
> But the hours are ours.

I fall and get up,
I burn and drown.
Have you only one body?

> Birds on the water,
> Dawn on the eyelids.

The marbles push forward,
Absorbed in themselves,
As tall as death.

> Are the palaces stranded?
> Whiteness drifting.

Women, children
On the roadways.
Scattered fruit.

Harapos o relámpagos?
Procesión en el llano.

Sonora y fresca
Por brazos y tobillos
Corre la plata.

Con un traje alquilado
El niño va a su boda.

La ropa limpia
Tendida entre las piedras.
Mírala y calla.

En el islote chillan
Monos de culo rojo.

Cuelga del muro,
Oscuro sol en celo,
Un avispero.

También mi frente es sol
De pensamientos negros.

Moscas y sangre.
En el patio de Kali
Trisca un cabrito.

Del mismo plato comen
Dioses, hombres y bestias.

Sobre el dios pálido
La diosa negra baila,
Decapitada.

Calor, hora rajada—
Y esos mangos podridos ...

Tu frente, el lago:
Lisos, sin pensamientos.
Salta una trucha.

Rags or lightning-bolts?
A parade on the black plain.

Cool silver
Gliding tinkling
On arms and ankles.

A small boy arrives at his wedding
In a rented suit.

Clean clothes
Spread out among the stones.
Look at them and be still.

Monkeys with red buttocks
Howling on the islet.

A wasp-nest hangs
From the wall, a dark
Furious sun.

My brow is also a sun
With black thoughts inside.

Flies. Blood.
A kid cavorts
In Kali's courtyard.

Gods, men and beasts
Eat from the same plate.

The headless black
Goddess dances
On the pallid god.

Heat, time split open—
And those rotted mangoes ...

Your brow. The lake.
Smooth, without thoughts.
A fish leaps.

Cae la tarde. Encienden
Luces sobre las aguas.

Ondulaciones:
Ocre el llano—y la grieta ...
Tu ropa al lado.

Sobre tu cuerpo en sombra
Estoy como una lámpara.

Viva balanza:
Los cuerpos enlazados
Sobre el vacío.

El cielo nos aplasta,
El agua nos sostiene.

Abro los ojos:
Nacieron muchos árboles
Hoy por la noche.

Esto que he visto y digo,
El sol, blanco, lo borra.

Twilight. Lights
On the water.

Ripples. The plain
Is ochre. So is the crevice . . .
Your clothes near by.

I am like a lamp
On your shadowed body.

Living scales:
Two bodies intertwined
Over the emptiness.

The sky crushes us.
The water sustains us.

I open my eyes.
A forest of trees
Was born tonight.

What I have seen, said, the
White sun erases.

[L.K.]

Felicidad en Herat

A Carlos Pellicer

Vine aquí
Como escribo estas líneas,
Sin idea fija:
Una mezquita azul y verde,
Seis minaretes truncos,
Dos o tres tumbas,
Memorias de un poeta santo,
Los nombres de Timur y su linaje.

Encontré al viento de los cien días.
Todas las noches las cubrió de arena,
Acosó mi frente, me quemó los párpados.
La madrugada:
                    Dispersión de pájaros
Y ese rumor de agua entre piedras
Que son los pasos campesinos.
(Pero el agua sabía a polvo.)
Murmullos en el llano,
Apariciones
                    Desapariciones,
Ocres torbellinos
Insustanciales como mis pensamientos.
Vueltas y vueltas
En un cuarto de hotel o en las colinas:
La tierra un cementerio de camellos
Y en mis cavilaciones siempre
Los mismos rostros que se desmoronan.
El viento, el señor de las ruinas,
Es mi único maestro?
Erosiones:
El menos crece más y más.

Happiness in Herat

For Carlos Pellicer

I came here
As I write these lines,
At random:
A blue-and-green mosque,
Six truncated minarets,
Two or three tombs,
Memories of a poet-saint,
The names of Timur and his lineage.

I met the wind of the hundred days.
It spread sand over all the nights.
It scourged my brow, scorched my lids.
Daybreak:
       Dispersion of birds
And that sound of water among stones
Which is the peasant's footsteps.
(But the water tasted of dust.)
Murmurs in the plain,
Appearances
       Disappearances,
Ochre whirlwinds
Insubstantial as my thoughts.
Wheeling and wheeling
In the hotel room, on the hills:
This land a camels' graveyard
And in my brooding
Always the same crumbling faces:
Is the wind, the lord of ruins,
My only master?
Erosions:
Minus grows more and more.

En la tumba del santo,
Hondo en el árbol seco,
Clavé un clavo,
           No,
Como los otros, contra el mal de ojo:
Contra mi mismo.
           (Algo dije:
Palabras que se lleva el viento.)

Una tarde pactaron las alturas.
Sin cambiar de lugar
           Caminaron los chopos.
Sol en los azulejos
           Súbitas primaveras.
En el Jardín de las Señoras
Subí a la cúpula turquesa.
Minaretes tatuados de signos:
La escritura cúfica, más allá de la letra,
Se volvió transparente.
No tuve la visión sin imágenes,
No ví girar las formas hasta desvanecerse
En claridad inmóvil,
El ser ya sin sustancia del sufí.
No bebí plenitud en el vacío
Ni ví las treinta y dos señales
Del Bodisatva cuerpo de diamante.
Ví un cielo azul y todos los azules,
Del blanco al verde
Todo el abanico de los álamos
Y sobre el pino, más aire que pájaro,
El mirlo blanquinegro.
Vi al mundo reposar en si mismo.
Vi las apariencias.
Y llamé a esa media hora:
Perfección de lo Finito.

At the saint's tomb
I nailed a nail
Deep into the lifeless tree,
                          Not,
Like the others, against the evil eye:
Against myself.
(I said something—
Words the wind took away.)

One afternoon the heights convened.
The poplars walked around
                          While standing still.
Sun on the glazed tiles
                    Sudden springtimes.
In the Ladies' Garden
I climbed to the turquoise cupola.
Minarets tattooed with characters:
That Cufic script became clear
Beyond its meaning.
I did not have the vision without images,
I did not see forms whirl till they disappeared
In immobile clarity,
In the Sufi's being-without-substance.
I did not drink plenitude in vacuity
Nor see the two and thirty signs
Of the Bodhisattva's diamond-body.
I saw a blue sky and all the shades of blue,
And the white to green
Of the spread fan of the poplars,
And, on the tip of the pine tree,
The black-and-white ouzel,
Less bird than air.
I saw the world resting upon itself.
I saw the appearances.
And I named that half-hour:
Perfection of the Finite.

[L.K.]

Juventud

El salto de la ola
    Más blanca
Cada hora
   Más verde
Cada día
   Más joven
La muerte

Youth

The leap of the wave
                    Whiter
Each hour
            Greener
Each day
            Younger
Death

[C.T.]

Lo idéntico

(Anton Webern, 1883–1945)

Espacios
  Espacio
Sin centro ni arriba ni abajo
Se devora y se engendra y no cesa
Espacio remolino
    Y caída hacia arriba
Espacios
  Claridades cortadas a pico
Suspendidas
   Al flanco de la noche
Jardines negros de cristal de roca
En una vara de humo florecidos
Jardines blancos que estallan en el aire
Espacios
  Un solo espacio que se abre
Corola
  Y se disuelve
Espacio en el espacio
    Todo es ninguna parte
Lugar de las nupcias impalpables

One and the same

(Anton Webern, 1883–1945)

Spaces
     Space
Without centre no above or below
Devours and engenders itself and does not cease
Whirlpool space
          And it falls into height
Spaces
     Clarities
Cut into jewel-points
            Hanging
From night's sheerness
Black gardens of rock crystal
Flowering along a bough of smoke
White gardens that explode in air
Spaces
     A sole space that unfolds
Flower-face
        And dissolves
Space into space
All is nowhere
Place of impalpable nuptials

[C.T.]

Furiosamente

Furiosamente
        Gira
Sobre un reflejo
          Cae
En línea recta
         Afilada
Blancura
      Asciende
Ya sangriento el pico
Sal dispersa
        Apenas línea
Al caer
    Recta
Tu mirada
       Sobre esta página
Disuelta

Furiously

Furiously
       It whirls round
Over a reflection
           Falls
In a straight line
           Clear-cut
Whiteness
       Ascends
The beak now blood-red
Scattered salt
         Scarcely a line
As it falls
       Straight
Your glance
        Over this page
Dissolved

                                     [C.T.]

Tumba del poeta

El libro
       El vaso
El verde oscuramente tallo
              El disco
La bella durmiente en su lecho de música
Las cosas anegadas en sus nombres
Decirlas con los ojos
             En un allá no se donde
Clavarlas
      Lámpara lápiz retrato
Esto que veo
        Clavarlo
Como un templo vivo
            Plantarlo
Como un árbol
        Un dios
Coronarlo
      Con un nombre
           Inmortal
Irrisoria corona de espinas
           Lenguaje!
El tallo y su flor inminente
           Sol-sexo-sol
La flor sin sombra
        En un allá sin donde
Se abre
     Como el horizonte
           Se abre
La extensión inmaculada
Transparencia que sostiene a las cosas
Caídas
     Por la mirada

Tomb of the poet

The book
        The glass
The green obscurely a stalk
                   The record
Sleeping beauty in her bed of music
Things drowned in their names
To say them with the eyes
                In a beyond I cannot tell where
Nail them down
          Lamp pencil portrait
This that I see
          To nail it down
Like a living temple
          Plant it
Like a tree
      A god
Crown it
      With a name
          Immortal
Derisible crown of thorns
             Speech!
The stalk and its imminent flower
            Sun-sex-sun
The flower without shadow
            In a beyond without where
Opens
     Like the horizon
           Opens
Immaculate extension
Transparency which sustains things
Fallen
     Raised up

Levantadas
        En un reflejo
              Suspendidas
Lunas multiplicadas
           En la estepa
Haz de mundos
         Instantes
Racimos encendidos
Selvas andantes de astros
Sílabas errantes
Milenios de arena cayendo sin término
                  Marea
Todos los tiempos del tiempo
               SER
Una fracción de segundo
           Lámpara lápiz retrato
En un aquí no se donde
         Un nombre
Comienza
      Asirlo plantarlo decirlo
Como un bosque pensante
          Encarnarlo
Un linaje comienza
        En un nombre
Un adán
     Como un templo vivo
Nombre sin sombra
        Clavado
Como un dios
      En este aquí sin donde
Lenguaje!
     Acabo en su comienzo
En esto que digo
      Acabo
SER
  Sombra de un nombre instántaneo

NUNCA SABRE MI DESENLACE

By the glance
                    Held
                              In a reflection
Moons multiplied
                              Across the steppe
Bundle of worlds
                              Instants
Glowing bunches
Moving forests of stars
Wandering syllables
Millennia of sand endlessly falling away
                                        Tide
All the times of time
                              TO BE
A second's fraction
                              Lamp pencil portrait
In a here I cannot tell where
                              A name
Begins
          Seize on it, plant, say it
Like a wood that thinks
                              Flesh it
A lineage begins
                    In a name
An adam
          Like a living temple
Name without shadow
                              Nailed
Like a god
          In this here-without-where
Speech!
          I cease in its beginning
In this that I say
                    I cease
TO BE
          Shadow of an instantaneous name

I SHALL NEVER KNOW MY BOND'S UNDOING

[C.T.]

Al pintor Swaminathan

Con un trapo y un cuchillo
                    Contra la idea fija
Contra el toro del miedo
Contra la tela contra el vacío
                    El surtidor
La llama azul del cobalto
                    El ámbar quemado
Verdes recién salidos del mar
                        Añiles reflexivos
Con un trapo y un cuchillo
                    Sin pinceles
Con los insomnios con la rabia con el sol
Contra el rostro en blanco del mundo
El surtidor
            La ondulación serpentina
La vibración acuática del espacio
El triángulo el arcano
La flecha clavada en el altar negro
Los alfabetos coléricos
La gota de tinta de sangre de miel
Con un trapo y un cuchillo
                    El surtidor
Salta el rojo mexicano
                    Y se vuelve negro
Salta el rojo de la India
                    Y se vuelve negro
Los labios ennegrecen
                    Negro de Kali
Carbón para tus cejas y tus párpados
Mujer deseada cada noche
                    Negro de Kali
El amarillo y sus fieras abrasadas

To the painter Swaminathan

With a rag and a knife
                 Against the idée fixe
The bull of fear
Against the canvas and the void
                    The uprushing spring
Blue flame of cobalt
                Burnt amber
Greens fresh from the sea
                 Minds' indigo
With a rag and a knife
                No brushes
With the insomnia the rage the sun
Against the blank face of the world
The uprushing spring
                  Serpentine undulation
The aquatic vibration of space
The triangle the arcanum
The arrow stuck on the black altar
The angry alphabet
The drop of ink of blood of honey
With a rag and a knife
                  The uprushing spring
Springs the Mexican red
              Turns black
The Indian red springs
              Turns black
The lips go black
              The black of Kali
Charcoal for your eyelids
Woman desired every night
                  The black of Kali
The yellow and its scorched beast

El ocre y sus tambores subterráneos
El cuerpo verde de la selva negra
El cuerpo azul de Kali
                    El sexo de la Guadalupe
Con un trapo y un cuchillo
                    Contra el triángulo
El ojo revienta
            Surtidor de signos
La ondulación serpentina avanza
Marea de apariciones inminentes

El cuadro es un cuerpo
Vestido sólo por su enigma desnudo

The ochre and its underground drums
The green body of the black jungle
The blue body of Kali
                    The sex of Guadalupe
With a rag and a knife
                    Against the triangle
The eye bursts
              Fountain of signs
The serpentine undulation moves
Wave upon wave of imminent apparitions

The canvas a body
Dressed in its own naked enigma

                              [J.S. and the author]

Lectura de John Cage

Leyendo
  Fluyendo
Music without measurements,
Sounds passing through circumstances.
Dentro de mí los oigo
    Pasar afuera
Fuera de mí los veo
    Pasar conmigo.
Yo soy la circunstancia.
Música:
  Oigo adentro lo que veo afuera
  Veo dentro lo que oigo fuera.
(No puedo oírme oír: Duchamp.)
    Soy
Una arquitectura de sonidos
Instantáneos
  Sobre
Un espacio que se desintegra.
    (Everything
We come across is to the point.)
    La música
Inventa al silencio,
    La arquitectura
Inventa al espacio.
    Fábricas de aire.
El silencio
  Es el espacio de la música:
Un espacio
  Inextenso:
    No hay silencio
Salvo en la mente.
  El silencio es una idea,

On reading John Cage

Reading
      Flowing
Music without measurements,
Sounds passing through circumstances.
I hear them within me
                  Outside they pass
I see them outside me
                  Within me they pass.
I am the circumstance.
Music:
      I hear within what I see outside
      I see within what I hear outside
(I can't hear myself hearing: Duchamp.)
                      I am
An architecture of sounds
Instantaneous
          On
A space that disintegrates itself
                (Everything
We come across is to the point.)
                  Music
Invents silence,
          Architecture
Invents space.
          Factories of air.
Silence
      Is the space of music:
Space
   Unextended:
            There is no silence
Save in the mind.
          Silence is an idea,

La idea fija de la música.
La música no es una idea:
Es sonido,
Sonidos caminando sobre el silencio.
(Not one sound fears the silence
That extinguishes it.)
Silencio es música
Música no es silencio.
Nirvana es Samsara
Samsara no es Nirvana.
El saber no es saber:
Recobrar la ignorancia,
Saber del saber.
No es lo mismo
Oir los pasos de esta tarde
Entre los árboles y las casas
Que
Ver la misma tarde ahora
Entre los mismos árboles y casas
Después de leer
Silence:
Nirvana es Samsara
Silencio es música.
(Let life obscure
The difference between art and life.)
Música no es silencio:
No es decir
Lo que dice el silencio,
Es decir
Lo que no dice.
Silencio no tiene sentido
Sentido no tiene silencio.
Sin ser oída
La música se desliza entre ambos.
(Every something is an echo of nothing.)
En el silencio de mi cuarto
El rumor de mi cuerpo:
Inaudito.
Un día oiré sus pensamientos.
La tarde

The idée fixe of music.
Music is not an idea:
It is sound,
Sounds walking over silence.
(Not one sound fears the silence
That extinguishes it.)
Silence is music
Music is not silence.
Nirvana is Samsara
Samsara is not Nirvana.
Knowing is not knowing:
Recovering ignorance,
Knowledge of knowing.
It is one thing to hear
These afternoon-footsteps
Between trees and houses
Another to see
Between same trees and houses
These afternoon-footsteps
After reading

Silence:
Nirvana is Samsara
Silence is music.
(Let life obscure
The difference between art and life.)
Music is not silence:
It is not saying
What silence says,
It is saying
What it doesn't say.
Silence has no sense
Sense has no silence.
Without being heard
Music slips between both.
(Every something is an echo of nothing.)
In the silence of my room
The murmur of my body:
Unheard.
One day I shall hear its thoughts.
The afternoon

Se ha detenido:
                    No obstante — camina.
Mi cuerpo oye al cuerpo de mi mujer
                              (A cable of sound)
Y le responde:
                    Esto se llama música.
La música es real,
                    El silencio es una idea.
John Cage es japonés
                              Y no es una idea:
Es sol sobre nieve.
                         Sol y nieve no son lo mismo:
El sol es nieve y la nieve es nieve
                              O
El sol no es nieve ni la nieve es nieve
O
   John Cage no es americano
(U.S.A. is determined to keep the Free World free,
U.S.A. determined)
                              O
John Cage es americano
                         (That the U.S.A. may become
Just another part of the world.
                         No more, no less.)
La nieve no es sol
                    La música no es silencio
El sol es nieve
                    El silencio es música
(The situation must be Yes-and-No
                              Not either-or)
Entre el silencio y la música
                              El arte y la vida
La nieve y el sol
                    Hay un hombre
Ese hombre es John Cage
                         (Committed
To the nothing in between)
                              Dice una palabra
No nieve no sol
                    Una palabra

Stands still:
                    Yet—it walks.
My body hears the body of my wife
                              (A cable of sound)
And responds to it:
                    This is called music.
Music is real,
              Silence is an idea.
John Cage is Japanese
                    And is not an idea:
He is sun on snow.
                    Sun and snow are not the same:
Sun is snow and snow is snow
                              Or
Sun is not snow and snow is not snow
Or
   John Cage is not American
(U.S.A. is determined to keep the Free World free,
U.S.A. determined)
                    Or
John Cage is American
                    (That the U.S.A. may become
Just another part of the world.
                         No more, no less.)
Snow is not sun
              Music is not silence
Sun is snow
              Silence is music
(The situation must be Yes-and-No
                         Not either-or)
Between silence and music
                    Art and life
Snow and sun
              There is a man
This man is John Cage
                    (Committed
To the nothing in between)
                    He says a word
Not snow not sun
              One word

Que no es
        Silencio:
A year from Monday you will hear it.

La tarde se ha vuelto invisible.

Which is not
        Silence:
A year from Monday you will hear it.

The afternoon has become invisible.

                            [M.F.W. and G.A.]

Carta a León Felipe

León
      El quinto signo del cielo giratorio
                                El león
Cara de sol
      El sol cara de hombre
                             Sol
El quinto son
        Al centro de la música
El quinto sol
        Centro del movimiento
                      León
Felipe querido
        Buenos días
Hoy llegó el sol con tu poema
              Hoy
Llegó el león
      Y se plantó enmedio
Entre los domos de los mausoleos Lodi
(Bajo el cielo intachable
              Negros
Planetas cercenados)
Y el Yamuna de fango iridiscente

En Prithviraj Road 13
            Leo tu poema
Como esta luz
       Natural
           En su palma
Los colores los cuerpos las formas
               Saltan
Reposan saltan
      Las cosas

Letter to León Felipe

León
        The fifth sign of the revolving sky
                                The lion
Sun-face
            The sun face of man
                                Sol
The fifth note
                In the centre of music
The fifth sun
                Centre of movement
                                        León
Felipe
        Good morning
Today the sun arrived with your poem
                                        Today
The lion came
                And stood fast-rooted midway
Between the mausoleums of the Lodis
(Under the blameless sun
                            Black
Chopped-off planets)
And the Jamuna of iridescent mud

In Prithviraj Road 13
                        I read your poem
Natural
        As this light
                    On its palm
Colours bodies forms
                        Leap
Rest leap
        The things

Como los saltimbanquis
                    Andan por el aire
Dos loros en pleno vuelo
                    Desafían al movimiento
Y al lenguaje
            Míralos
                Ya se fueron!
Irradiación de unas cuantas palabras
Es un aleteo
            El mundo se aclara
Sólo para volverse invisible

Aprender a ver oír decir
                        Lo instantáneo
Es nuestro oficio
                Fijar vértigos?
Las palabras
            Como los pericos en celo
Se volatilizan
                Su movimiento
Es un regreso a la inmovilidad

No nos queda dijo Bataille
Sino escribir comentarios
                        Insensatos
Sobre la ausencia de sentido del escribir
Comentarios que se borran
                        La escritura poética
Es borrar lo escrito
                Escribir
Sobre lo escrito
                Lo no escrito
Representar la 'comedia' sin desenlace
Je ne puis parler d'une absence de sens
Sinon lui donnant un sens qu'elle n'a pas

La escritura poética es
                    Aprender a leer
El hueco de la escritura
                    En la escritura

Like acrobats
                  Go through the air
Two parrots in open flight
                  Defy movement
And language
                  See them
                           Already gone!
Irradiation of a few words
A flapping of wings
                  The world becomes clearer
Only to turn invisible again

Learning to see to hear to say
                           The instantaneous
Is our trade
                  Fixing vertigoes?
The words
                  As these parakeets in heat
Dissipate themselves
                           Their movement
A return to immobility

All that remains for us, said Bataille,
Is to write commentaries
                           Senseless
On the absence of sense of writing
Commentaries that erase themselves
                                 To write poetry
Is to erase the written
                  To write
On what is written
                  The unwritten
To represent the 'comedy' without denouement
Je ne puis parler d'une absence de sens
Sinon lui donnant un sens qu'elle n'a pas

To write poetry
                  Is learning to read
The hole of writing
                  In the writing

No huellas de lo que fuimos
                    Caminos
Hacia lo que somos
                    El poeta
Lo dices en tu carta
                    Es el preguntón
El que dibuja la pregunta
                    Sobre el hoyo
Y al dibujarla
                    La borra
La poesía
                    Es la ruptura instantánea
Instantáneamente cicatrizada
                    Abierta de nuevo
Por la mirada de los otros
                    La ruptura
Es la continuidad
La muerte del Comandante Guevara
También es ruptura
                    No un fin
Su memoria
                    No es una cicatriz
Es una continuidad que se desgarra
Para continuarse
                    La poesía
Es la hendidura
                    El espacio
Entre una palabra y otra
Configuración del inacabamiento

León Felipe
                    Ando
Por un jardín que tú no conoces
Y hablo contigo conmigo
                    Cae
Sobre este verdor hipnotizado
Una luz impalpable
                    Implacable
Cae
    Sobre las letras de tu poema

132

Not the footprints of what we were
                              The paths
Towards what we are
                    The poet
You say it in your letter
                         Is the questioner
He who draws the question
                         On the hole
And while drawing it
                    Erases it
Poetry
      Is instant rupture
Instantly healed
                Torn open again
By the reading of others' eyes
                             Rupture
Is continuity
The death of Commander Guevara
Is also rupture
                Not an end
His memory
          Is not a scar
It is a continuity that tears itself
For continuing itself
                      Poetry
Is the fissure
              The space
Between one word and another
The configuration of the unaccomplished

León Felipe
           I walk
In a garden that you have not walked
And speak with you with myself
An impalpable light
                    Falls
Implacable
          On this hypnotized green
It falls
        On the letters of your poem

Sobre el gato sonámbulo
Sobre el insecto de vidrio
Sobre el pájaro carbonizado en su canto
Sobre la piel de mi mujer dormida-despierta
El cuerpo femenino
                    Es una pausa
Terrible
          Proximidad inaccesible
La demasía de la presencia
                              Fija
Y no obstante
              Desbordante
                            Un arco
De agua que al tocar la otra orilla
Se vuelve aire
               Ondulación
Delicia de planicie que se despliega
Hasta anegarse
               Hasta negarse

Esta luz es natural
                    Ignora la muerte
Nos ignora
          Adiós
Buenos días León Felipe
No nos vimos en México
El desencuentro fué un encuentro
Irradiación de unas cuantas palabras
Una ligereza de sílabas girando
En la inmovilidad de este día de invierno.

On the somnambulant cat
On the insect of glass
On the bird carbonized while singing
On the skin of my wife sleeping awake
The female body
                    Is a pause
Terrible
          Proximity inaccessible
An excess of presence
                    Fixed
Yet
    Overflowing
                    An arch
Of water that turns into air
On touching the other shore
                            Undulation
Delight of the plains unfolding
Until it drowns
                    Denies itself

This light is natural
                    It ignores death
It ignores us
                Adiós
Good morning León Felipe
We didn't meet in Mexico
The non-meeting was an encounter
Irradiation of a few words
A lightness of turning syllables
In the immobility of this winter day.

                                    [G.A. and the author]

Aparición

Si el hombre es polvo
Esos que andan por el llano
Son hombres

Apparition

If man is dust
Those who go through the plain
Are men

[C.T.]

Madurai

En el bar del British Club
—Sin ingleses, *soft drinks*—
Nuestra ciudad es santa y cuenta
Me decía, apurando su naranjada,
Con el templo más grande de la India
(Mainakshi, diosa canela)
Y el garage T.S.V.
                  (tus ojos son dos peces)
El más grande también en el subcontinente:
Sri K. J. Chidambaram,
Yo soy familiar de ambas instituciones.
Director de The Great Lingam Inc.,
Compañía de Autobuses de Turismo.

Madurai

In the bar at the British Club
—soft drinks, no Englishmen—
Our city is holy and rates high
                              he told me,
sucking up the last of his orangeade,
with the largest temple in India
(Minakshi, cinnamon goddess:)
and the T.S.V. Garage,
                              (your eyes are two fishes)
also the biggest in the subcontinent:
Sri K. J. Chidambaram,
I am connected with both institutions.
Director of The Great Lingam Inc.,
a bus company specializing in tourists.

[P.B.]

Vrindaban

Rodeado de noche
Follaje inmenso de rumores
Grandes cortinas impalpables
Hálitos
  Escribo me detengo
Escribo
  (Todo está y no está
Todo calladamente se desmorona
Sobre la página)
    Hace unos instantes
Corría en un coche
Entre las casas apagadas
    Corría
Entre mis pensamientos encendidos
Arriba las estrellas
    Jardines serenísimos
Yo era un árbol y hablaba
Estaba cubierto de hojas y ojos
Yo era el murmullo que avanza
El enjambre de imágenes
(Ahora trazo unos cuantos signos
Crispados
  Negro sobre blanco
Diminuto jardín de letras
A la luz de una lámpara plantado)
Corría el coche
Por los barrios dormidos yo corría
Tras de mis pensamientos
    Míos y de los otros
Reminiscencias supervivencias figuraciones

Vrindaban

Surrounded by night
Immense forest of breathing
Vast impalpable curtains
Murmurs
            I write
I stop
        I write
                (All is and is not
And it all falls apart on the page
In silence)
                A moment ago
A car raced down the street
Among the extinguished houses
                        I raced
Among my lighted thoughts
Above me the stars
                    Such quiet gardens
I was a tree and spoke
Was covered with leaves and eyes
Was the rumour pushing forward
A swarm of images
(I set down now a few
Twisted strokes
                Black on white
Diminutive garden of letters
Planted in the lamp's light)
The car raced on
Through the sleeping suburb
                        I raced
To follow my thoughts
                    Mine and others
Reminiscences Left-overs Imaginings

Nombres
>Los restos de las chispas
>Y las risas de la velada
>La danza de las horas
>La marcha de las constelaciones

Y otros lugares comunes
Yo creo en los hombres
>>O en los astros?

Yo creo
>(Aquí intervienen los puntos
Suspensivos)
>Yo veo

Pórtico de columnas carcomidas
Estatuas esculpidas por la peste
La doble fila de mendigos
>Y el hedor

Rey en su trono
>Rodeado
Como si fuesen concubinas
Por un vaivén de aromas
Puros casi corpóreos ondulantes
Del sándalo al jazmín y sus fantasmas
Putrefacción
>Fiebre de formas
>>Fiebre del tiempo
En sus combinaciones extasiado
Cola de pavo real el universo entero
Miríadas de ojos
>>En otros ojos reflejados
Modulaciones reverberaciones de un ojo único
Un solitario sol
>Oculto
Tras su manto de transparencias
Su marea de maravillas
Todo llameaba
>Piedras mujeres agua
Todo se esculpía
>Del color a la forma

Names
      The remains of sparks
      The laughter of the late parties
      The dance of the hours
      The march of the constellations
And other commonplaces
Do I believe in man
                Or in the stars?
I believe
      (With here a series
Of dots)
      I see

A portico of weather-eaten pillars
Statues carved by the plague
It is a double line of beggars
                The stench
A king on his throne
            Surrounded
By a coming and going of aromas
As if they were concubines
Pure almost corporeal undulating
From the sandalwood to the jasmine
And its phantoms
          Fever of forms
            Fever of time
Ecstatic in its combinations
The whole universe a peacock's tail
Myriads of eyes
          Other eyes reflecting
Modulations
        Reverberations of a single eye
A solitary sun
         Hidden
Behind its cloth of transparencies
Its tide of marvels
Everything was flaming
              Stones women water
Everything sculptured
         From colour to form

De la forma al incendio
                    Todo se desvanecía
Música de metales y maderas
En la celda del dios
                    Matriz del templo
Música de soles enlazados
                              Música
Como el agua y el viento en sus abrazos
Y sobre las materias que gemían
Confundidas
                La voz humana
Luna en celo por el mediodía
Queja del alma que se desencarna
(Escribo sin conocer el desenlace
De lo que escribo
                         Busco entre líneas
Mi imagen es la lámpara
                              Encendida
En mitad de la noche)
                         Saltimbanqui
Mono de lo Absoluto
                         Garabato
En cuclillas
                Cubierto de cenizas pálidas
Un sadú me miraba y se reía
Desde su orilla me miraba
                         Lejos lejos
Como los animales y los santos me miraba
Desnudo desgreñado embadurnado
Un rayo fijo los ojos minerales
Yo quise hablarle
Me respondió con borborigmos
                              Ido ido
Adónde
        A qué región del ser
A qué existencia a la intemperie de qué mundos
En qué tiempo?
                    (Escribo
Cada letra es un germen

From form to fire
                    Everything was vanishing
Music of wood and metal
In the cell of the god
                    Womb of the temple
Music like spliced suns
                    Music
Like the wind and water embracing
And over the confused moans
Of matter
          The human voice
A moon in heat at midday
Complaint of the disembodied soul
(I write without knowing the outcome
Of what I write
                I look between the lines
My image is the lamp
                    Lit
In the middle of the night)
                        Mountebank
Ape of the absolute
                    Cowering
Pothook
        Covered with pale ashes
A sadhu looked at me and laughed
Watching me from the other shore
                            Far off, far off
Watching me like the animals like the saints
Naked   uncombed   smeared
A fixed ray a mineral glitter his eyes
I wanted to speak to him
He answered with a rumble of bowels
                            Gone   gone
Where?
        To what region of being
To what existence
                    In the open air of what worlds
In what time?
                (I write
Each letter is a germ

La memoria
Insiste en su marea
Y repite su mismo mediodía)
Ido ido
          Santo pícaro santo
Arrobos del hambre o de la droga
Tal vez vio a Krishna
                    Arbol azul y centelleante
Nocturno surtidor brotando en la sequía
Tal vez en una piedra hendida
Palpó la forma femenina
                    Y su desgarradura
El vértigo sin forma
                Por esto o aquello
Vive en el muelle donde queman a los muertos

Las calles solas
Las casas y sus sombras
Todo era igual y todo era distinto
El coche corría
            Yo estaba quieto
Entre mis pensamientos desbocados
(Ido ido
Santo payaso santo mendigo rey maldito
Es lo mismo
            Siempre lo mismo
                        En lo mismo
Es ser siempre en sí mismo
                        Encerrado
En lo mismo
            En sí mismo cerrado
Idolo podrido)
            Ido ido
Desde su orilla me miraba
                    Me mira
Desde su interminable mediodía
Yo estoy en la hora inestable
El coche corre entre las casas
Yo escribo a la luz de una lámpara
Los absolutos las eternidades

The memory
Imposes its tide
And repeats its own midday)
Gone   gone
          Saint   scoundrel   saint
In beatitudes of hunger or drugs
Perhaps he saw Krishna
                    Sparkling blue tree
Dark fountain splashing amid the drought
Perhaps in a cleft stone
He grasped the form of woman
                              Its rent
The formless dizziness
                    For this or that
He lives on the ghat where they burn the dead

The lonely streets
The houses and their shadows
All was the same and all different
The car raced on
                    I was quiet
Among my runaway thoughts
(Gone   gone
Saint   clown   saint   beggar   king   damned
It is the same
              Always the same
                              Within the same
It is to be always within oneself
Closed up in the same
                    Closed up on oneself
Rotted idol)
          Gone   gone
He watched me from the other shore
                              He watches me
From his interminable noon
I am in the wandering hour
The car races on among the houses
I write by the light of a lamp
The absolutes the eternities

Y sus aledaños
                No son mi tema
Tengo hambre de vida y también de morir
Sé lo que creo y lo escribo
Advenimientos del instante
                        El acto
El movimiento en que se esculpe
Y se deshace el ser entero
Conciencia y manos para asir el tiempo
Soy una historia
                Una memoria que se inventa
Nunca estoy solo
Hablo siempre contigo Hablas siempre conmigo
A oscuras voy y planto signos

Their outlying districts
                    Are not my theme
I am hungry for life and for death also
I know what I know and I write it
The embodiment of time
                    The act
The movement in which the whole being
Is sculptured and destroyed
Consciousness and hands to grasp the hour
I am a history
                A memory inventing itself
I am never alone
I speak with you always
                        You speak with me always
I move in the dark
                I plant signs

[L.K.]

Viento entero

El presente es perpetuo
Los montes son de hueso y son de nieve
Están aquí desde el principio
El viento acaba de nacer
                        Sin edad
Como la luz y como el polvo
                        Molino de sonidos
El bazar tornasolea
                        Timbres motores radios
El trote pétreo de los asnos opacos
Cantos y quejas enredados
Entre las barbas de los comerciantes
Alto fulgor a martillazos esculpido
En los claros de silencio
                        Estallan
Los gritos de los niños
                        Príncipes en harapos
A la orilla del río atormentado
Rezan orinan meditan
                        El presente es perpetuo
Se abren las compuertas del año
                        El día salta
        Agata
        El pájaro caído
Entre la calle Montalambert y la de Bac
Es una muchacha
                        Detenida
Sobre un precipicio de miradas
Si el agua es fuego
                        Llama
En el centro de la hora redonda
                        Encandilada

Wind from all compass points

The present is motionless
The mountains are of bone and of snow
They have been here since the beginning
The wind has just been born
                          Ageless
As the light and the dust
                          A windmill of sounds
The bazaar spins its colours
                          Bells   motors   radios
The stony trot of dark donkeys
Songs and complaints entangled
Among the beards of the merchants
The tall light chiselled with hammer-strokes
In the clearings of silence
                    Boys' cries
        Explode
Princes in tattered clothes
On the banks of the tortured river
Pray   pee   meditate
                          The present is motionless
The floodgates of the year open
                    Day flashes out

          Agate
      The fallen bird
Between rue Montalambert and rue de Bac
Is a girl
        Held back
At the edge of a precipice of looks
If water is fire
              Flame
              Dazzled
In the centre of the spherical hour

                    Potranca alazana
Un haz de chispas
                    Una muchacha real
Entre las casas y las gentes espectrales
Presencia chorro de evidencias
Yo ví a través de mis actos irreales
La tomé de la mano
                         Juntos atravesamos
Los cuatro espacios los tres tiempos
Pueblos errantes de reflejos
Y volvimos al día del comienzo
El presente es perpetuo
                         21 de junio
Hoy comienza el verano
                              Dos o tres pájaros
Inventan un jardín
                         Tú lees y comes un durazno
Sobre la colcha roja
                    Desnuda
Como el vino en el cántaro de vidrio
                         Un gran vuelo de cuervos
En Santo Domingo mueren nuestros hermanos
'Si hubiera parque no estarían ustedes aquí'
                    Nosotros nos roemos los codos
En los jardines de su alcázar de estío
Tipú Sultán plantó el árbol de los jacobinos
Luego distribuyó pedazos de vidrio
Entre los oficiales ingleses prisioneros
Y ordenó que se cortasen el prepucio
Y se lo comiesen
                         El presente es perpetuo
El sol se ha dormido entre tus pechos
La colcha roja es negra y palpita
Ni astro ni alhaja
                    Fruta
Tú te llamas dátil
                    Datia
Castillo de sal si puedes

A sorrel filly
A marching battalion of sparks
                        A real girl
Among wraithlike houses and people
Presence a fountain of reality
I looked out through my own unrealities
I took her hand
                Together we crossed
The four quadrants the three times
Floating tribes of reflections
And we returned to the day of beginning
The present is motionless
                        June 21st
Today is the beginning of summer
                                Two or three birds
Invent a garden
                You read and eat a peach
On the red couch
                Naked
Like the wine in the glass pitcher
                                A great flock of crows
Our brothers are dying in Santo Domingo
'If we had the munitions
                You people would not be here'
        We chew our nails down to the elbow
In the gardens of his summer fortress
Tipoo Sultan planted the Jacobin tree
Then distributed glass shards among
The imprisoned English officers
And ordered them to cut their foreskins
And eat them
                The present is motionless
The sun has fallen asleep between your breasts
The red covering is black and heaves
Not planet and not jewel
                        Fruit
You are named
                Date
                Datia
Castle of Leave-If-You-Can

                    Mancha escarlata
Sobre la piedra empedernida
Galerías terrazas escaleras
Desmanteladas salas nupciales
Del escorpión
                    Ecos repeticiones
Relojería erótica
                    Deshora
                         Tú recorres
Los patios taciturnos bajo la tarde impía
Manto de agujas en tus hombros indemnes
Si el fuego es agua
                         Eres una gota diáfana
La muchacha real
                    Transparencia del mundo
El presente es perpetuo
                         Los montes
        Soles destazados
Petrificada tempestad ocre
                         El viento rasga
              Ver duele
El cielo es otro abismo más alto
Garganta de Salang
La nube negra sobre la roca negra
El puño de la sangre golpea
                    Puertas de piedra
Sólo el agua es humana
En estas soledades despeñadas
Sólo tus ojos de agua humana
                    Abajo
En el espacio hendido
El deseo te cubre con sus dos alas negras
Tus ojos se abren y se cierran
                         Animales fosforescentes
Abajo
        El desfiladero caliente
La ola que se dilata y se rompe
                    Tus piernas abiertas

                    Scarlet stain
Upon the obdurate stone
Corridors
                Terraces
                            Stairways
Dismantled nuptial chambers
Of the scorpion
                        Echoes repetitions
The intricate and erotic works of a watch
                                    Beyond time
                                        You cross

Taciturn patios under the pitiless afternoon
A cloak of needles on your untouched shoulders
If fire is water
                You are a diaphanous drop
The real girl
                    Transparency of the world
The present is motionless
                            The mountains
                Quartered suns
Petrified storm earth-yellow
                            The wind whips
                                    It hurts to see
The sky is another deeper abyss
                            Gorge of the Salang Pass
Black cloud over black rock
Fist of blood strikes
                        Gates of stone
Only the water is human
In these precipitous solitudes
Only your eyes of human water
                            Down there
In the cleft
Desire covers you with its two black wings
Your eyes flash open and close
                            Phosphorescent animals
Down there
            The hot canyon
The wave that stretches and breaks
                            Your legs apart

El salto blanco
La espuma de nuestros cuerpos abandonados
              El presente es perpetuo
El morabito regaba la tumba del santo
Sus barbas eran más blancas que las nubes
Frente al moral
                  Al flanco del torrente
Repetiste mi nombre
                        Dispersión de sílabas
Un adolescente de ojos verdes te regaló
Una granada
              Al otro lado del Amu-Darya
Humeaban las casitas rusas
El son de la flauta usbek
Era otro río invisible y más puro
En la barcaza el batelero estrangulaba pollos
El país es una mano abierta
                        Sus líneas
        Signos de un alfabeto roto
Osamentas de vacas en el llano
Bactriana
              Estatua pulverizada
Yo recogí del polvo unos cuantos nombres
Por esas sílabas caídas
Granos de una granada cenicienta
Juro ser tierra y viento
                    Remolino
Sobre tus huesos
                El presente es perpetuo
La noche entra con todos sus árboles
Noche de insectos eléctricos y fieras de seda
Noche de yerbas que andan sobre los muertos
Conjunción de aguas que vienen de lejos
Murmullos
              Los universos se desgranan
Un mundo cae
                  Se enciende una semilla
Cada palabra palpita
                        Oigo tu latir en la sombra

The plunging whiteness
The foam of our bodies abandoned
                              The present is motionless
The hermit watered the saint's tomb
His beard was whiter than the clouds
Facing the mulberry
                    On the flank of the rushing stream
You repeat my name
                    Dispersion of syllables
A young man with green eyes presented you
With a pomegranate
                    On the other bank of the Amu-Darya
Smoke rose from Russian cottages
The sound of an Usbek flute
Was another river invisible clearer
The boatman
                    On the barge was strangling chickens
The countryside is an open hand
                              Its lines
                    Marks of a broken alphabet
Cow skeletons on the prairie
Bactria
          A shattered statue
I scraped a few names out of the dust
By these fallen syllables
Seeds of a charred pomegranate
I swear to be earth and wind
                              Whirling
Over your bones
                    The present is motionless
Night comes down with its trees
Night of electric insects and silken beasts
Night of grasses which cover the dead
Meeting of waters which come from far off
Rustlings
          Universes are strewn about
A world falls
              A seed flares up
Each word beats
              I hear you throb in the shadow

Enigma en forma de reloj de arena
                    Mujer dormida
Espacio espacios animados
Anima mundi
              Materia maternal
Perpetua desterrada de sí misma
Y caída perpetua en su entraña vacía
                              Anima mundi
Madre de las razas errantes
                    De soles y de hombres
Emigran los espacios
              El presente es perpetuo
En el pico del mundo se acarician
Shiva y Parvati
              Cada caricia dura un siglo
Para el dios y para el hombre
                    Un mismo tiempo
Un mismo despeñarse
              Lahor
                    Río rojo barcas negras
Entre dos tamarindos una niña descalza
Y su mirar sin tiempo
                    Un latido idéntico
Muerte y nacimiento
Entre el cielo y la tierra suspendidos
Unos cuantos álamos
Vibrar de luz más que vaivén de hojas
                    Suben o bajan?
El presente es perpetuo
                    Llueve sobre mi infancia
Llueve sobre el jardín de la fiebre
Flores de sílex árboles de humo
En una hoja de higuera tú navegas
Por mi frente
              La lluvia no te moja
Eres la llama de agua
                    La gota diáfana de fuego
Derramada sobre mis párpados

158

A riddle shaped like an hour-glass
                              Woman asleep
Space   living spaces
Anima mundi
               Maternal substance
Always torn from itself
Always falling into your empty womb
                                   Anima mundi
Mother of the nomadic tribes
                         Of suns and men
The spaces turn
               The present is motionless
At the top of the world
Shiva and Parvati caress
                         Each caress lasts a century
For the god and for the man
                         An identical time
An equivalent hurling headling
                         Lahore
                              Red river black boats
A barefoot girl
               Between two tamarinds
And her timeless gaze
                    An identical throbbing
Death and birth
A group of poplars
Suspended between sky and earth
They are a quiver of light more than a trembling of leaves
                         Do they rise
                              Or fall?
The present is motionless
                         It rains on my childhood
It rains on the feverish garden
Flint flowers   trees of smoke
In a fig-leaf you sail
                    On my brow
The rain does not wet you
You are flame of water
                         The diaphanous drop of fire
Spilling upon my eyelids

Yo veo a través de mis actos irreales
El mismo día que comienza
                              Gira el espacio
Arranca sus raíces el mundo
No pesan más que el alba nuestros cuerpos
                              Tendidos

I look out through my own unrealities
The same day is beginning
                              Space wheels
The world wrenches up its roots
Our bodies
              Stretched out
                              Weigh no more than dawn

[P.B.]

Contigo

Ráfagas turquesa
Loros fugaces en parejas
                              Vehemencias
El mundo llamea
                    Un árbol
Hirviente de cuervos
Arde sin quemarse
                           Quieta
Entre los altos tornasoles
                              Eres ~
Una pausa de la luz
                       El día
Es una gran palabra clara
Palpitación de vocales
                            Tus pechos
Maduran bajo mis ojos
                            Mi pensamiento
Es más ligero que el aire
                            Soy real
Veo mi vida y mi muerte
El mundo es verdadero
Veo
    Habito una transparencia

With you

Gusts of wind turquoise
Parrots fleeing in pairs
           Vehemence
The world flames
        A tree
Seething with crows
Blazes without burning
          You are
Quiet among the tall sunflowers
             Are
A pause of the light
        The day
Is a great clear word
Palpitation of vowels
          Your breasts
Ripen under my eyes
        My thought
Is lighter than the air
        I am real
I see my life and my death
The world is true
        I see
I inhabit a transparency

                                                [L.K.]

Ejemplo

El trueno anda por el llano
El cielo esconde todos sus pájaros
Sol desollado
    Bajo su luz final
Las piedras son más piedras

Rumor de follajes inciertos
Como ciegos que buscan su camino
Dentro de unos instantes
Noche y agua serán un solo cuerpo

Example

Thunder crosses the plain
The sky hides all its birds
Flayed sun
             The stones under
Its last light are stonier

Murmur of uncertain foliage
Like blind men seeking their way
In a few moments
Night and water will be one body

[L.K.]

Pasaje

Más que aire

        Más que agua

Más que labios

        Ligera ligera

Tu cuerpo es la huella de tu cuerpo

Transit

Lighter than air

        Than water

Than lips

     Light light

Your body is the footprint of your body

                       [L.K.]

Cauce

Oye la palpitación del espacio
Son los tambores del verano
Los pasos de la estación en celo
Sobre las brasas del año
Es su ruido de alas y de crótalos
La crepitación de la tierra
Bajo su vestidura de insectos y raíces
La sed se despierta y construye
Sus grandes jaulas de vidrio
Allí cantas tu canción furiosa
Tu canción dichosa
            De agua encadenada
Allí cantas desnuda
Con los pechos y el vientre manchados
Con la cara manchada de polen
Sobre el paisaje abolido
Tu sombra es un país de pájaros
Que el sol dispersa con un gesto

River-bed

Hear the palpitation of space
The drums of summer
                              The footfalls
Of the season in heat
That sound above the year's ashes
Is of wings and rattles
The crepitation of the earth
Under its raiment of insects and roots
Thirst awakens and builds
Its great glass cages
You sing your furious song there
Your joyous song of
                              Chained waters
You sing naked there
With your breasts and belly smeared
With your face smeared with pollen
Your shadow on the abolished landscape
Is a land of birds
Which the sun scatters with a gesture

[L.K.]

Cima y gravedad

Hay un árbol inmóvil
Hay otro que avanza
    Un río de árboles
Golpea mi pecho
    Es la dicha
El oleaje verde
Tú estás vestida de rojo
      Eres
El sello del año abrasado
El tizón carnal
    El astro frutal
En ti como sol
    La hora reposa
Sobre un abismo de claridades
La altura se nubla de pájaros
Sus picos construyen la noche
Sus alas sostienen al día
Plantada en la cresta de la luz
Entre la fijeza y el vértigo
    Tú eres
   La balanza diáfana

Summit and gravity

There is a motionless tree
There is another advancing
                            A river of trees
Beats at my breast
                        The green surge
Is good fortune
                    You are
The seal of the burnt-out year
The carnal firebrand
                            The fruitlike star
I eat the sun in you
                        The hour rests
Above an abyss of clarities
The height is clouded with birds
Their bills construct the night
Their wings sustain the day
Standing on the crest of the light
Between fixity and vertigo
            You are
The diaphanous balance

[L.K.]

Presente

Sobre la reverberación de la piedra
                                Salina vertical
La violencia azul petrificada
                       El caer incesante
De la cortina
              (Atrás
El sol combate con el mar)
                     El piso de ladrillo
Respirado respirante
                 La ventana la mesa el lecho
Ahora el azul se tiende se extiende
                         Sostiene
Una almohada rosada Una muchacha
El vestido lacre todavía caliente
                    Los ojos
Entrecerrados no por la espera
                    Por la visitación
Está descalza
             La plata tosca enlaza
Refresca
        Un brazo desnudo
Sobre sus pechos valientes baila el puñal del sol
En el vientre
             Eminencia inminencia
Una línea de hormigas negras
                    Vibración
De un cuerpo un alma un color
De la miel quemada
             La miel negra
Al centelleo de la amapola
La amapola negra
           Abres
Los ojos
       Eres un sol sediento

Now

Over the reverberations of the wall
                              Vertical salt-pan
Petrified blue violence
                    Incessant fall
Of the curtain (Behind it
The sun battles the sea)
                         The tile floor
Breathes in breathes out
                         The window table bed
Now the blue stretches extends
                              Sustains
A rose pillow A girl
Her dress burnt lac still warm
                              Eyes
Half-closed not from expectation
                              For the visitation
She is barefoot
                  The unpolished silver
Entwines and cools her naked arm
The dagger of the sun dances on her valiant breasts
On her belly
                  Eminence imminence
A line of black ants
                    Vibration
Of a body a soul a colour
From the burnt honey
                    The black honey
To the scintillation of the poppy
The black poppy
                  When you open your eyes
You are a thirsty sun

[L.K.]

Blanco
(1966)

NOTE

Blanco: the colour white; blank left in writing; void, emptiness; mark to shoot at (blank: the central white spot of a target); aim, object or desire.

Blanco is a composition which allows the following variant readings:

(*a*) in its totality, as a single text;

(*b*) the central column, with the exclusion of those to the left and right, is a poem whose theme is that of the passage of the word from silence before speech to silence after it;

(*c*) the left-hand column is a love poem, divided into four moments which correspond to the four traditional elements;

(*d*) the right-hand column is another poem, counterpointing the erotic one and composed of four variations on sensation, perception, imagination and understanding;

(*e*) each one of the four parts made up of the two columns can be read, without worrying about previous divisions, as a single text: four independent poems.

(*f*) the central column can be read as six isolated texts and the right- and left-hand columns as eight.

y passion the world is bound, by
assion too it is released.

The Hevajra Tantra

Avec ce seul objet dont le Néant
s'honore.

Stéphane Mallarmé

el comienzo
            el cimiento
la simiente
            latente
la palabra en la punta de la lengua
inaudita   inaudible
            impar
grávida   nula
            sin edad
la enterrada con los ojos abiertos
inocente   promiscua
            la palabra
sin nombre   sin habla

Sube y baja,
Escalera de escapulario,
El lenguaje deshabitado.
Bajo la piel de la penumbra
Late una lámpara.
                    Superviviente
Entre las confusiones taciturnas,
                            Asciende
En un tallo de cobre
                    Resuelto
En un follaje de claridad:
                        Amparo
De caídas realidades.
                    O dormido
O extinto,
            Alto en su vara
(Cabeza en una pica),
                    Un girasol

Blanco

By passion the world is bound, by
passion too it is released.
The Hevajra Tantra

Avec ce seul objet dont le Néan
s'honore.

Stéphane Mallarm

the fountain
            the founding
the seed
        latent
word on the tip of the tongue
unheard   unhearable
                indivisible
gravid   void
            ageless
she they buried with open eyes
innocent   promiscuous
            the word
nameless   speechless

It ascends descends
Stairs of the mine-shaft.
Uninhabited language:
Under penumbra's skin
A lamp throbbing.
                    Survivor
Among taciturn confusions,
                            It ascends
On a copper stalk
                Dissolved
In a foliage of clarity,
                    Refuge
Of fallen realities.
                    Asleep
Or extinct,
            High on its pole
(Head on a pike)
                A sunflower

Ya luz carbonizada
                    Sobre un vaso
De sombra.
                En la palma de una mano
Ficticia,
            Flor
Ni vista ni pensada:
                        Oída,
Aparece
        Amarillo
Cáliz de consonantes y vocales
Incendiadas.

en el muro la sombra del fuego   *llama rodeada de leones*
en el fuego tu sombra y la mía   *leona en el circo de las llamas*
                                    ánima entre las sensaciones
el fuego te desata y te anuda
Pan Grial Ascua   *frutos de luces de bengala*
            Muchacha   *los sentidos se abren*
tú ríes—desnuda   *en la noche magnética*
en los jardines de la llama
            La pasión de la brasa compasiva

Un' pulso, un insistir,
Oleaje de sílabas húmedas.
Sin decir palabra
Oscurece mi frente
Un presentimiento de lenguaje.
Patience patience
(Livingston en la sequía)
River rising a little.
El mío es rojo y se agosta
Entre sableras llameantes:
Castillas de arena, naipes rotos
Y el jeroglífico (agua y brasa)

Already carbonized light
                              Above a glass
Of shadow.
                    In the palm of a hand
Fictitious,
                Flower
Neither seen nor thought:
                              Heard,
It appears
                Yellow
Calyx of consonants and vowels
All burning.

on the wall the shadow of the fire   *flame surrounded by lions*
in the fire your shadow and mine   *lioness in the circus of flames*
                                                  soul among sensations

the fire unties and ties you
Bread Grail Ember   *firework fruits*
                          Girl   *the senses are opening*
you laugh—naked   *in the magnetic night*
in the gardens of the flame
                    Passion of the compassionate ember

A pulse, an insistence,
Swell of humid syllables.
Without uttering a word
A presentiment of language
Darkens my forehead.
Patience patience
(Livingston in the drought)
River rising a little.
Mine is red and is scorched up
Among blazing sand-hills,
Sand-castles of Spain, torn pack of cards
And the hieroglyph (water and embers)

En el pecho de México caído.
Polvo soy de aquellos lodos.
Río de sangre,
                    Río de historias
De sangre,
            Río seco:
Boca de manantial
Amordazado
Por la conjuración anónima
De los huesos,
Por la ceñuda peña de los siglos
Y los minutos:
                    El lenguaje
Es una expiación,
                    Propiciación
Al que no habla,
                    Emparedado
Cada día
            Asesinado,
El muerto innumerable.
                            Hablar
Mientras los otros trabajan
Es pulir huesos,
                    Aguzar
Silencios
            Hasta la transparencia,
Hasta la ondulación,
                    El cabrilleo,
Hasta el agua:

los ríos de tu cuerpo   *el río de los cuerpos*
país de latidos   *astros infusorios reptiles*
entrar en ti   *torrente de cinabrio sonámbulo*
país de ojos cerrados   *oleaje de las genealogías*
agua sin pensamientos   *juegos conjugaciones juglarías*
entrar en mí   *subyecto y obyecto abyecto y absuelto*
al entrar en tu cuerpo   *río de soles*

Fallen on the breast of Mexico.
I am the dust of that mud.
Blood river,
                    River of histories
Of blood,
            Dry river:
Mouth of the source
Muzzled
By the anonymous conspiracy
Of bones,
By the grim rock of centuries
And minutes:
                    Language
Is an expiation,
                    Propitiation
To him who does not speak,
                            Immured,

Each day
            Assassinated,
The dead, one and innumerable.
                                To speak

While the others work
Is to polish bones,
                    To sharpen
Silences
        To the point of transparency,
To undulation,
                The foaming,
To water:

The rivers of your body
land of heart-beats
entering you
land of closed eyes
thoughtless water
entering me
while entering your body

the river of bodies
stars infusoria reptiles
torrent of somnambulant vermilion
tide of genealogies
games conjugations juggleries
subject and object abject and absolved
river of suns

país de espejos en vela
país de agua despierta
en la noche dormida

'las altas fieras de la piel luciente'
rueda el río seminal de los mundos
el ojo que lo mira es otro río

Me miro en lo que miro
como entrar por mis ojos
en un ojo más límpido
me mira lo que miro

Es mi creación esto que veo
la percepción es concepción
agua de pensamientos
soy la creación de lo que veo

delta de brazos del deseo
en un lecho de vértigos

agua de verdad
            verdad de agua

La transparencia es todo lo que queda

Paramera abrasada
Del amarillo al encarnado
La tierra es un lenguaje calcinado.
Hay púas invisibles, hay espinas
En los ojos.
            En un muro rosado
Tres buitres ahítos.
No tiene cuerpo ni cara ni alma,
Está en todas partes,
A todos nos aplasta:
                        Este sol es injusto.
La rabia es mineral.
                        Los colores
Se obstinan.
                Se obstina el horizonte.
Tambores tambores tambores.
El cielo se ennegrece
                        Como esta página.
Dispersión de cuervos.
Inminencia de violencias violetas.
Se levantan los arenales,
La cerrazón de reses de ceniza.
Mugen los árboles encadenados.
Tambores tambores tambores

land of mirrors in vigil
land of water awake
in the sleeping night

'the tall beasts of glittering hide'
the worlds' seminal river flows
the eye that sees it is another river

I see myself in what I see
like entering through my eyes
into another more limpid eye
what I see looks at me

It is my creation I see
perception is conception
water of thoughts
I am the creation of what I see

delta of the arms of desire
in a bed of vertigo

water of truth
truth of water

All that remains is transparency

Charred moorland
From yellow to flesh colour
Earth is a burnt-out language.
There are invisible prongs, there are
Thorns in the eyes.
                    On a pink wall
Three surfeited vultures.
It has no body, nor face nor soul,
It is everywhere,
It crushes us all:
                    This sun is unjust.
Rage is mineral.
                    The colours
Are obstinate,
                    Obstinate the horizon.
Drums drums drums.
The sky blackens
                    Like this page.
Dispersion of crows.
Imminence of violet violences.
Sands arise,
Darkness of beasts of ashes.
Trees roar in their chains.
Drums drums drums

Te golpeo cielo
                    Tierra te golpeo
Cielo abierto tierra cerrada
Flauta y tambor centella y trueno
Te abro te golpeo
                    Te abres tierra
Tienes la boca llena de agua
Tu cuerpo chorrea cielo
Tremor
              Tu panza tiembla
Tus semillas estallan
                    Verdea la palabra

se desata se esparce *árida ondulación*
se levanta se erige Idolo *entre brazos de arena*
desnuda como la mente *brilla se multiplica se niega*
en la reverberación del deseo *renace se escapa se persigue*
girando girando *visión del pensamiento gavilán*
en torno a la idea negra *cabra en la peña hendida*
el vellón de la juntura *paraje desnudo*
en la mujer desnuda *snap-shot de un latido de tiempo*
pirausta nudo de presencias *real irreal quieto vibrante*
inmóvil bajo el sol inmóvil *pradera quemada*
del color de la tierra *color de sol en la arena*
la yerba de mi sombra *sobre el lugar de la juntura*
mis manos de lluvia *oscurecida por los pájaros*
sobre tus pechos verdes *beatitud suficiente*
mujer tendida *hecha a la imagen del mundo*
                    El mundo haz de tus imágenes

Del amarillo al rojo al verde,
Peregrinación hacia las claridades,

I beat you sky
                    Earth I beat you
Open sky closed earth
Flute and drum lightning and thunder
I tear you open I beat you
                              You are opening
Earth your mouth full of water
Your body dripping with sky
Tremor
            Your belly trembles
Your seeds burst
                        The word grows green

unfastens itself spreads *arid undulation*
rises erects itself into an Idol *between arms of sand*
naked as the mind *gleams multiplies and denies itself*
in the reverberation of desire *is reborn escapes pursues itself*
swirling swirling *vision of the sparrow-hawk thought*
around the black idea *goat over the rock's cleft*
the fleece of the juncture *naked place*
in the naked woman *snapshot of a beat of time*
fiery butterfly knot of presences *real unreal quiet vibrant*
still beneath the stillness of the light *burnt plains*
of earth's colour *colour of sun on sand*
the grass of my shadow *over the place of the juncture*
my hands of rain *darkened by the birds*
on your green breasts *sufficient beatitude*
spread-out woman *made in the world's image*
            The world a bundle of your images

From yellow to red to green,
Pilgrimage towards clarities,

La palabra se asoma a remolinos
Azules.
  Gira el anillo beodo,
Giran los cinco sentidos
Alrededor de la amatista
Ensimismada.
    Traslumbramiento:
No pienso, veo
    —No lo que veo,
Los reflejos, los pensamientos veo.
Las precipitaciones de la música,
El número cristalizado.
Un archipiélago de signos.
Aerofanía,
   Boca de verdades,
Claridad que se anula en una sílaba
Diáfana como el silencio:
No pienso, veo
    —No lo que pienso,
La cara en blanco del olvido,
El resplandor de lo vacío.
Pierdo mi sombra,
    Avanzo
Entre los bosques impalpables,
Las esculturas rápidas del viento,
Los sinfines,
    Desfiladeros afilados,
Avanzo,
   Mis pasos
     Se disuelven
En un espacio que se desvanece
En pensamientos que no pienso.

caes de tu cuerpo a tu sombra *no allá sino en mis ojos*
en un caer inmóvil de cascada *cielo y suelo se juntan*
caes de tu sombra a tu nombre *intocable horizonte*
te precipitas en tus semejanzas *yo soy tu lejanía*

The word appears out of the blue
Of whirlpools.
                    The drunken ring whirls round,
The five senses whirl
About the amethyst
Self-gathered.
                    Splendour:
I do not think, I see
                        —Not what I see,
I see reflections, thoughts.
The precipitations of music,
Number crystallized.
An archipelago of signs.
Diaphaneity,
                Mouth of truths,
Clarity that abolishes itself in a syllable
Limpid as silence:
I do not see, I think
                        —Not what I think
Blank face of forgetfulness,
The radiance of the void.
I lose my shadow,
                    I advance
Among impalpable woods,
Rapid sculptures of the wind,
                        Along the endless,
Sharp-edged paths
                    I move,
My steps
            Dissolve
In a space that vanishes
In thoughts I do not think.

you fall from your body into your shadow *not there but in my eyes*
with the motionless fall of a cascade *sky and earth unite*
you fall from your shadow into your name *untouchable horizon*
you plunge yourself in your resemblances *I am your distance unfolding*

caes de tu nombre a tu cuerpo *el más allá de la mirada*
en un presente que no acaba *las imaginaciones de la arena*
caes en tu comienzo *las disipadas fábulas del viento*
derramada en mi cuerpo *yo soy la estela de tus erosiones*
tú te repartes como el lenguaje *espacio dios descuartizado*
tú me repartes en tus partes *altar el pensamiento y el cuchillo*
vientre teatro de la sangre *eje de los solsticios*
yedra arbórea lengua tizón de frescura *el firmamento es macho y hembra*
temblor de tierra de tu grupa *testigos los testículos solares*
lluvia de tus talones en mi espalda *falo el pensar y vulva la palabra*
ojo jaguar en espesura de pestañas *espacio es cuerpo signo pensamiento*
la hendidura encarnada en la maleza *siempre dos sílabas enamoradas*
los labios negros de la profetisa *A d i v i n a n z a*
entera en cada parte te repartes *las espirales transfiguraciones*
tu cuerpo son los cuerpos del instante *es cuerpo el tiempo el mundo*
visto tocado desvanecido *pensamiento sin cuerpo el cuerpo imaginario*

contemplada por mis oídos　　　　*Horizonte de música tendida*
olida por mis ojos　　　　　　　*Puente colgante del color al aroma*
acariciada por mi olfato　　　　　*Olor desnudez en las manos del aire*
oída por mi lengua　　　　　　　*Cántico de los sabores*
comida por mi tacto　　　　　　　*Festín de niebla*

habitar tu nombre　　　　　　　*Despoblar tu cuerpo*
caer en tu grito contigo　　　　　*Casa del viento*
　　　　　　La irrealidad de lo mirado
　　　　　　Da realidad a la mirada

　　　　　　En el centro
　　　Del mundo del cuerpo del espíritu
　　　La grieta　　　　El resplandor
　　　　　　No

you fall from your name into your body *the beyond of seeing*
into an unending present *imaginings of sand*
you fall into your very beginning *the scattered fables of the wind*
overflowing into my body *I am the stela of your erosions*
parts of your self you divide as speech *space carved out god*
me you divide in your gift of parts *the thought altar and knife*
belly theatre of blood *axis of solstices*
arboreal ivy tongue firebrand of coolness *the firmament is male and female*
earth tremor of your buttocks *witnesses are the solar testicles*
rain of your heels on my back *thought is phallus vulva the word*
eye jaguar in density of eyelashes *space is body sign thought*
the rose-coloured rent in the thicket *always two syllables in love*
the black lips of the prophetess *Riddle*
in each part of you you give yourself whole *spirals transfigurations*
the bodies of the instant are your body *time is body world is body*
seen touched vanished *bodiless thought the imaginary body*

contemplated by my hearing	*Expanding horizon of music*
tasted by my eyes	*Hanging bridge from colour to aroma*
caressed by my scent	*Odour nakedness in the hands of air*
heard by my tongue	*Canticle of flavours*
eaten by my touch	*Feast of mist*

to inhabit your name	*To dissipate your body*
to fall in your cry with you	*House of wind*

The unreality of the seen
Makes real the seeing

In the centre
Of the world the body the spirit
The crevice   The dazzle
No

En el remolino de las desapariciones
El torbellino de las apariciones
                    Sí
  El árbol de los nombres
                                No
Es una palabra
                    Sí
Es una palabra
                    Aire son nada
Son
    Este insecto
Revoloteando entre las líneas
De la página
                Inacabada
                        Inacabable
El pensamiento
                Revoloteando
Entre estas palabras
                    Son
Tus pasos en el cuarto vecino
Los pájaros que regresan
El árbol *nim* que nos protege
                            Los protege
Sus ramas acallan al trueno
Apagan al relámpago
En su follaje bebe agua la sequía
Son
    Esta noche
                (Esta música)
Mírala fluir
                Entre tus pechos caer
Sobre tu vientre
                Blanca y negra
Primavera nocturna
                    Jazmín y ala de cuervo
Tamborino y *sitar*
                No y Sí
Juntos
        Dos sílabas enamoradas

In the whirlpool of disappearances
The whirlwind of appearances
                    Yes
The tree of names
                    No
Is a word
            Yes
Is a word
            They are air nothing
They are
            This insect
Hovering among the lines
Of this page
            Unfinished
                        Unfinishable
The thought
            Hovering
Among these words
                    They are
Your steps in the next room
The birds that return
The *neem* tree that protects us
                        Protects them
Its branches hush the thunder
Quench the lightning
Drought drinks water in its foliage
They are
            This night
                        (This music)
See it flowing
                    Pouring between your breasts
Over your belly
                    White and black
Nocturnal spring
                    Jasmine and crow's wing
Small drum and sitar
                        No and yes
Together
            Two syllables in love

Si el mundo es real
                    La palabra es irreal
Si es real la palabra
                    El mundo
Es la grieta el resplandor el remolino
No
    Las desapariciones y las apariciones
                                        Sí

El árbol de los nombres
                    Real irreal
Son palabras
            Aire son nada
El habla
        Irreal
Da realidad al silencio
                        Callar
Es un tejido de lenguaje
                        Silencio
Sello
    Centelleo
                En la frente
En los labios
                Antes de evaporarse
Apariciones y desapariciones
La realidad y sus resurrecciones
El silencio reposa en el habla

El espíritu
Es una invención del cuerpo
El cuerpo
Es una invención del mundo
El mundo
Es una invención del espíritu
No   Sí
    Irrealidad de lo mirado
La transparencia es todo lo que queda
Tus pasos en el cuarto vecino

If the world is real
                    The word is unreal
If the word is real
                    The world
Is the crevice   the dazzle   the whirlwind
No
The disappearances and the appearances
                                        Yes
The tree of names
                    Real unreal
Are words
          They are air nothing
Speech
        Unreal
It lends reality to silence
                            Stillness
Is a fabric of language
                        Silence
Seal
    Spark
            On the forehead
On the lips
            Before evaporating
Appearances and disappearances
Reality and its resurrections
Silence reposes in speech

The spirit
Is an invention of the body
The body
An invention of the world
The world
An invention of the spirit
No   Yes
    Unreality of the seen
All that remains is transparency
Your steps in the next room

El trueno verde
                    Madura
En el follaje del cielo
                         Estás desnuda
Como una sílaba
                    Como una llama
Una isla de llamas
Pasión de brasa compasiva
El mundo
              Haz de tus imágenes
Anegadas en la música
                         Tu cuerpo
Derramado en mi cuerpo
                         Visto
Desvanecido
              Da realidad a la mirada

The green thunder
                    Ripens
In the foliage of the sky
                    You are naked
As a syllable
            As a flame
An island of flames
Passion of compassionate embers
The world
            a bundle of your images
Drowned in music
                    Your body
Flowing through my body
                            Seen
Vanished
            It makes real the seeing

[C.T. and G.A.]

Notes

SUN STONE

The symbols of the Aztec Calendar for Day 4 *Olín* (Movement) and Day 4 *Ehécatl* (Wind) appear at the beginning and end of *Sun Stone* respectively. The ancient Mexicans measured the synodical period of the planet Venus—which for them was one of the manifestations of the god Quetzalcoatl, the Plumed Serpent—from the Day 4 Olín, and the Day 4 Ehécatl marked, 584 days later, the conjunction of the planet and the sun: end of a cycle and beginning of another. *Sun Stone* is made up of 584 verses of eleven syllables.

SOLO FOR TWO VOICES

'*Mundicas/Those that carry the mundum*': the *mundum* was the basket of breads, etc., offered to Ceres in April; from this word was derived the Spanish *monda*, or gift of different kinds of bread and beeswax offered to Our Lady of the Meadow at Easter, or, elsewhere, to Our Lady of the Rock on St John's Day. The maidens who carried the offering were called *mondigas* (*mundicas*).

USTICA

Ustica is a volcanic desert island in the Sicilian sea. It was a Saracen graveyard.

THE BALCONY

'the Chinese poet' is Lin Yu (937–978).
'*Measures of a strange and wandering song*': first verse of the Dedication to *Soledades* by Góngora.

THE MAUSOLEUM OF HUMAYUN

Humayun (1530–56): son of Babur, conqueror of India and father of Akbar the Great.

196

THE DAY IN UDAIPUR

'A small boy arrives at his wedding/in a rented suit': there is a stall in the Udaipur bazaar where the bridegrooms, children belonging to the rural castes, hire the sumptuous costumes traditionally required for wedding ceremonies.

'A kid cavorts/In Kali's courtyard': the sacrifice of kids takes place in temples devoted to the goddess Kali.

HAPPINESS IN HERAT

'Memories of a poet-saint': the Sufi mystic and theologian Hazrat Khwaja Abdullah Ansar. There is an almost withered tree in the garden which surround his tomb. Devotees drive iron nails into the tree to prevent or cure the evil eye and, above all, toothache.

'the turquoise cupola': on the mausoleum of Gahar Shad, the wife of Shah Rakh, the son of Timur, Governor of Herat.

'the two and thirty signs': according to the Mahayana sutras, certain signs appear on the bodies of Bodhisattvas, usually thirty-two in number.

ON READING JOHN CAGE

Cage's books are *Silence* (1961) and *A Year from Monday* (1967). The italicized quotations are from the latter.

'Nirvāṇa is Saṃsāra/Saṃsāra is not Nirvāṇa': in Mahayana Buddhist literature, we find the formula: *Nirvāṇa is Saṃsāra, Saṃsāra is Nirvāṇa* which sums up one of the central ideas of the Madhyamika school: the ultimate identity of phenomenal and transcendental reality, of the world of reincarnation and the void (*śūnyatā*).

LETTER TO LEÓN FELIPE

First stanza: *León*, name of a person and an animal (*lion* in English); *sol*, the *sun* and the fifth note of the musical scale (G:sol); 'El quinto sol', el 'Centro del movimiento' refers, in the Aztec cosmology, to the Fifth Age of the world.

'*Fixing vertigoes?*': Rimbaud in *Alchimie du Verbe*.

Quotations from Georges Bataille are from *L'Expérience Intérieure*.

VRINDABAN

'sadhu': a wandering ascetic.

'blue tree': the god Krishna is blue and black.

'Perhaps in a cleft stone/He groped the form of woman': certain stones are symbols of the Great Goddess, particularly those whose form suggests a vulva (*yoni*).

'Gone gone': the expression 'Gone, gone to the Other Shore' figures frequently in the Prajñāpā ramitā Sutras.

WIND FROM ALL COMPASS POINTS

'Un gran vuelo de cuervos': Rubén Darío in *Cantos de Vida y Esperanza*.

'If we had the munitions/You people would not be here': Mexican school history-books attribute this statement to General Anaya when he gave up the Plaza de Churubusco to General Scott, head of the U.S. troops which invaded Mexico in 1847.

'Tipoo Sultan planted the Jacobin tree': the facts referred to here are historical.

'Datia': in the walled city of the name, in Madhya Pradesh, there is a palace-castle also called Datia. Built on a black, craggy promontory it towers over the city and the plain. According to Fergusson, it is the finest example of palace architecture in the seventeenth century. Built to the orders of a condottiere in the service of the Emperor Jahangir, Datia has never been lived in, except by bats and snakes: its owner was assassinated before he could take possession and since then no one else has dared to try. The perfect geometry of its patios, galleries and terraces evokes not so much the castles of de Sade as the circular rigour of his thought. A stone solipsism corresponds to a solipsism in words.

'In a fig-leaf you sail': allusion to the children's tale *Almendrita*.